Eternal Damnation
on Trial

Daniel A. Schinzing

Eternal Damnation on Trial, by Daniel L. Schinzing
ISBN # 0- 9635597-0-2

Copyright ©, 1993,
by Daniel L. Schinzing
ALL RIGHTS RESERVED

Published By **Impact Books, Inc.** for
Daniel L. Schinzing
P. O. Box 2003,
Cleburne, TX 76031

Cover Design: Lion & The Lamb, Mansfield, TX

Scripture quotations are taken from the New King James Version.
Copyright © 1979, 1980, 1982 by Thomas Nelson, Inc.
Used by permission.

Printed in the United States of America

DEDICATION

This book is dedicated to my parents, Ruth and Al Schinzing, New Baltimore, Michigan, who gave me the basics of Christianity when I was young. And now that I am old, I have not departed from it.

Also, this book is dedicated to my Uncle, and best friend the past several years, Harold Hovdenes, Lewisville, Texas. He supported me when he thought I was right, but also let me know when he thought I was full of it.

There may have been better people than these three who have lived in the world, but probably not many.

ACKNOWLEDGEMENTS

My first thank you is to my wife of fourteen years, Nancy Lee Dimeis Schinzing, for putting up with my disorganized, scholarly, contrarian ways. I am still praying for her to see our marriage as a loving adventure, rather than her cross to bear.

To my daughter Danielle Lee: If she is not the greatest daughter in the history of the world, she ranks right up there. In my eyes she is almost perfect and being her father is a better experience than I ever thought fatherhood would be.

To my secretary who prefers to remain nameless, I greatly appreciate her extra work on the computer to get this book completed and a special thank you to her husband, Howard Carley, for putting up with her nights and weekends when I give her time off.

To my friends, Mark and Denise Munchrath (No, I did not make up that name.) for doing the cover and giving me free professional advice. They own Lion and Lamb Advertising in Mansfield, Texas.

To Pam Adams and Teri Lyons, my neighbor, who helped tremendously with the editing process.

To Dave Padgett, Arlington Property Services. my associate and competitor, for sharing an office with a last born, and for sharing his computer expertise.

To my friends and associates who encouraged me in this process and allowed me to think they actually liked me: Susan Tankersley, Jimmy Haines, Steve and Lisa Roye, Oliver Whitfield, Eric Dillon, Rory, Flora, and Sasil Smithee, John and Jeanine Davis, Jay Poe, Wendell Cason and Mac Ledbetter.

And to my in-laws, Dolores and Jerry Dimeis, for being smart enough to encourage their daughter to consider marrying me and for not foreclosing on me several years back.

TABLE OF CONTENTS

AUTHOR'S PREFACE

In November of 1981, I was fired for the only time in my life. That was just nine weeks after moving to Dallas, Texas, where I had come in search of my fortune, I thought this was the lowest point in my 28 years; then I knew I was at the bottom when I was unable to find employment within a month. Three years earlier, I was on the fast track to being one of the best sports officials ever. I had my sights set on the NBA until the board governing high school athletics in Missouri decided to suspend me for a year because of insubordination. That was the end of the dream.

From the bottom, the only way I could go was up, but I had no idea which direction that was. Grasping at straws, with my wife working, I decided to attend Bible School at the same time I searched for employment. Never having had a desire to be a preacher, I was not sure of what I was doing at a Bible School, but the Bible was opening up to me as it never had before.

I would walk the one and a half miles to school every day and then back again, refusing to ride with a fellow student who drove a bright yellow and black sports car. One afternoon, I decided to take him up on a ride home. We began discussing our future ministries. He talked more than I did because I had no clue where I was headed. His parting words to me that day were, "I can't wait to read your first book." Say What?!! It shocked me, but I didn't doubt it at all. After all, I had a propensity for spouting off my opinion and often putting it on paper. But to put a cover on it, and to try to convince people it is worth spending their hard earned money on is another mountain to climb.

Well, with this lump of paper you are holding in your hand, I am on the way up that mountain. If I can get 1999 other people to buy this book, then my wife will feel as if I made it over that mountain. As for me, I would like to see more sales than that. Maybe somewhere between the 2000 of this first printing and launching a new major religion. That is ridiculous! You are right, Christianity is the ultimate religion. Right? Which Christianity? Which one of the 300-plus "Christianities" is the true religion?

The purpose of this book is to lay out in simple language what the Bible says on the subject of eternal damnation in a form that can easily be understood by anyone with a 5th grade education.

I have yet to find a church or denomination that correctly teaches this subject as it is written in the Bible. That is not to say that there are none that teach it correctly. If there is anyone out there who believes what is written in this book, I hope they write to my wife and my mother-in-law, so that the two of them will no longer think I am somewhat nutty. Don't bother writing to my mother in Michigan, because she will love me no matter what. Mothers are like that. But my mother-in-law in Solvay, NY, is yet to be convinced that I am on the right track with this subject.

If you do continue to read this book, I would like to warn you about something. When you finish it, you will not be able to look at your belief system the same way you look at it today. That will hold true if you are honest with yourself. A truly honest person is always seeking truth and I believe that is what you will find in the Bible.

Many years ago, my decision to find out if the Bible really did contain the word of God, the Creator of the universe, was an honest attempt on my part to discover the truth. As my brother, Dwayne, pointed out to me several years ago, my motivation in life has always been to be right. When I am wrong, I will admit that I am wrong and accept the truth. Regarding this subject of eternal damnation I have been totally honest with the reader. Whenever I learned something new, I informed the reader and I held nothing back.

Does that mean I am right about every bit of evidence supporting my premise? Not at all. My premise is correct, but not every point of my argument is infallible. I have done the best research and study that I could with the resources I had available at the time. If you have any suggestions, then I am humble enough to accept your instruction. Just do not come to me with more eternal damnation theology, as it is a false religion.

In Bible School, a classmate and I were always bouncing our theology off one another. We finally came to the conclusion that the whole world was forgiven, but they had to accept it. A year later we moved from Dallas to Cleburne to work with Believers Word Center Ministry. Within a few months the leader, Jim Myers, had convinced me that everyone was forgiven, a few months later he changed his mind. He even went so far as to say that "either everyone is going to make it or almost no one will make it."

About September 1984, I left that group and for a while I was without a church body. I knew I could not go back to the "eternal damnation theology" because I knew too much. When I look back now, I seemed to know only two things: That Jesus' covenant had paid the price for all the world's sin, and that no matter what my wife did to me, there was no way that I would want her (my only close loved one at the time) separated from me for eternity. At the time, I had no evidence to prove either. That is all I knew. It wasn't much, was it?

What I learned in the next four years was enough to fill a book, which I did in 1988. I finished this book in December 1988, but I could not find a publisher. So, I have decided to have about 2000 copies printed in an attempt to convince more than ten people that the Creator of this universe is a whole lot better than people give Him credit. The idea that God has something against unbelievers is a lie from Satan!! The Bible contains absolutely no evidence to support an eternal damnation theology, as will be shown to you in the last part of this book.

One of the main reasons that people taught such a theology is because they never defined the terms used in the Bible. Had they just picked up a dictionary or studied the Greek and Hebrew languages from which the Bible was translated, they would have known better. Had they studied the history of covenants, they would have understood the immense love that the Creator of the universe has for us.

Knowing what Jesus' covenant did for us was the beginning of my knowledge. Shortly after beginning my research, I came across *two very important principles* which I had not heard before. The first was: *Where there is no law, there is no transgression.* In other words, you cannot break a law which is not there. For eternal damnation theology to be valid, the Bible must specifically teach that each person must accept Jesus as Savior in order to receive forgiveness of sins. The Bible specifically teaches that forgiveness is a free gift. [Romans 4:15, 5:13, Hebrews 7:12]

Principle number two: *A person's unbelief will not affect the faithfulness of God.* [Romans 3:3-4]. "For what if some did not believe? Will their unbelief make the faithfulness of God without effect? Certainly not!" How can a person's unbelief affect what God has already done?

By the time I had concluded my research, I had discovered fifteen different ways to debunk the eternal damnation theology. Some of them were found simply by finding the true definition of the words, grace, atone-ment, reconciliation, propitiation, justification, forgive-ness, Savior, transgression, redemption, justice, and covenant. Then I read the Word, as it was written, in each passage, and I discovered that people had not been reading it for what it said, but for what they wanted it to say. Then I threw in the four proofs: *faithfulness of God, the faith of Jesus, no law = no transgression,* and *the fact that Jesus died for our sins.* That leaves me with approx-imately two hundred verses opposing the "eternal damna-tion theology."

I came to find out the evidence on the side of eternal damnation theology is only circumstantial and would not hold up in any court of justice. Which is how I got the title "*Eternal Damnation on Trial.*" I just want to lay out the facts for everyone to see and that is what I have done. I do not care who is offended by the facts, "whose ox gets gored," or whose ministry is hurt by what the Word says. I can only demonstrate my love and service to everyone by teaching the Word as it was written.

I have made an honest attempt to give credit to other authorities and publishers when I took a quote from their work. If you discover any oversight on my part, please notify me of the needed correction and if other printings follow, I will make the corrections or give credit. I encourage the readers to purchase almost all of the works I quote from, especially *Dake's Annotated Reference Bible; The New King James Version; The Amplified Bible; The Blood Covenant,* by H. Clay Trumbull; and *Jesus, Rabbi and Lord,* by Robert L.

Lindsey. It is my opinion that your library is not complete without these books.

My heart-felt desire is that you take your time getting through this book, as there is a lot of information contained in it. Be of an open mind and you will see your life changing for the better as you come into a new understanding of the Creator of the Universe and His Son, our Savior, our covenant Partner, Jesus Christ.

ETERNAL DAMNATION THEOLOGY

IS WORLDWIDE

Sally[1] sat on her government issue bed leaning against a wall of the cubicle she had to share with another girl. This cubicle, one of many in this juvenile home for girls, had been Sally's home for three years. By some people's standards, Sally had been a problem child, resulting in her virtual imprisonment at the home. She had been crying in that position for hours when her roommate, Patty, returned to find her there. When questioned, Sally related that she was crying because she was convinced she was on her way to "hell."

Sally had an abortion before being placed in the home, and having been raised as a Roman Catholic, she was programmed to believe that eternal punishment awaited her. Believing nothing could be done about it, her life demonstrated what was inside her mind. She lived in torment because she believed what she had always been told.

----

1. The names in the examples have been altered to protect the privacy of the individuals.

Antonio Luigi[1] had spent his entire life believing that he had to take communion just before he died. Antonio, 78 years old, lay in a hospital bed close to death. As the family awaited word of his final passing, Antonio pulled the life sustaining tubes, got out of bed, and collapsed outside while trying to reach his church. He was programmed to believe that he had to take communion just before death, or else he would spend eternity in hell. He had lived in fear every day that God was going to punish him for any sins not forgiven by the priest. What a way to live!

Did you see Robert DeNiro in the movie, "The Mission,"[2] when he played the role of a slave trader, turned murderer, turned Jesuit priest candidate? In order to pay penance for his sins, he dragged a huge net-load of soldier's armor through the jungle. The priests accompanying him only encouraged him to pay penance rather than enlightening him on what the Bible had to say about sins and paying penance. After one of his former enemies cut the rope that released him from his bondage, it appeared that he felt he had paid the penance for his sins and was therefore forgiven. Keep in mind, he did not feel forgiven until he had done something to gain the forgiveness.

A large number of Christian children of the United States are collecting "Precious Moments" dolls, toys, clothes, books, and other paraphernalia. In the "Precious Moments" book, *Bible Stories*, there is a chapter, "God Punishes Sin." "The Bible tells us that God will punish us for our sins. We all sin. You do. I do. Our punishment will be living far away from God and His love."

----

1. Ibid

2. (1986, Warner Bros.)

16

These are scary words for a little child just beginning to learn about God.

In 1077 A.D., the emperor of the Holy Roman Empire, Henry IV, was excommunicated by Pope Gregory after a power struggle between the two men. Accompanying the excommunication was the declaration that all of Henry's subjects no longer had to pay allegiance to him, leaving Henry on his way to everlasting damnation without anyone to follow him. To save himself from "hellfire," and his kingdom from anarchy, Henry decided it would be in his best interest to get absolution (forgiveness of sins) from Pope Gregory. In order to obtain this forgiveness, Henry had to cross the Alps in the middle of winter to arrive at the Pope's closed door, where he stood barefoot for three days in penitential attire. All that, so that he could get forgiveness for his sins and not spend eternity in hell fires. (*Great Religions Of The World,* National Geographic Society, 1971, p. 341.)

While still a teenager, I asked my father, a Pentecostal pastor, to clarify his teaching on hell and who would be there. I asked him a question something like this: "If a person commits a minor little sin just before he dies, without an opportunity to ask God's forgiveness, even if he had been a Christian all his life, where will he spend eternity?" His reply was that the person definitely would go to "hell," whether it is a major sin or a minor sin. In God's eyes, they are all the same.

The Hindus believe each soul, or "atman," strives through successive rebirths to ascend the scale of merit until--after a life of rectitude, self-control, non-violence, charity, reverence for all living creatures, and devotion to ritual--it wins liberation from worldly existence to achieve union with Brahman, "the Supreme Being." (*Great Religions,* p. 37) Hinduism preached a salvation through knowledge that was only given to a chosen few. (*Great Religions,* p. 91.)

Siddhartha Gautama was disillusioned with Hinduism and its rituals and caste system, so he came up with his own religion called Buddhism. He decreed a path of spiritual improvement based on such things as avoidance of ill will, malicious talk, lust, and hurt to living things. The path stressed mindful concentration--insight through meditation--in gaining understanding...It unseals the eyes of the spirit, leads to peace of mind, to knowledge, to enlightenment, to "nirvana." To attain nirvana, or infinity, a Buddhist must escape the wheel of rebirth, meaning that unless people shed the cravings and wrong inclinations of life, they are going to come back in a new life and will continue coming back until they get it right. (*Great Religions,* p. 94-95)

The newest of the world's major religions is Islam with its own way to salvation. "Therefore invoke not with Allah another god, lest thou be one of the doomed." (*Great Religions,* p. 229)

The Koran taught that rich must share with poor, promised a glorious afterlife for the righteous and hellfire for others. Mohammed's early writings, or "suras," describe the position of Islam on eternal damnation. "Nay, I swear by the Day of Resurrection...on that day man will cry: Whither to flee? Alas! No refuge! Unto thy Lord is the recourse that day. Vivid images color the passages. A trumpet blast signals the resurrection. The dead rise. Informed of their good and evil deeds as recorded in the book of life, they pass onto a bridge. The righteous cross safely into eternal bliss in lush "gardens underneath rich rivers flow." Evildoers are hurled into the abyss where "garments of fire will be cut out for them; boiling fluid...poured down on their heads." (*Great Religions,* p. 231.)

Christianity sprang from Judaism, but the beliefs are quite different. "The beliefs that Judaism teaches do not constitute a creed upon the acceptance of which the Jew may find salvation. Fundamentally, Judaism stresses conduct rather than profession and offers considerable latitude in the matter of belief. God is the Savior of all souls, helping men to be delivered from ignorance, sinfulness, hate, and lust. But salvation is not achieved solely by an act of God; God requires man's cooperation in the process." (*Collier's Encyclopedia,* The Crowell-Collier Publishing Co., Vol. 9 pg. 62, Vol. 13, pg. 656.)

"Judaism declares that no one can stand between God and man; that there is no need for mediation or intervention. Therefore, the Jew rejects vicarious (substitutionary) atonement, holding that every man is directly responsible to God for his sins. Though bound by laws of cause and effect, and at times hampered by social and political forces, man still has the freedom of will to make moral decisions.

"Man should not serve God for reward, but God, who is just, will reward the righteous, if not here and now, then in the life hereafter. Judaism affirms the immortality of man's soul...as to the character of Paradise or Heaven where the righteous are rewarded, and of Hell or Gehenna, where the wicked are punished, Jews have differing interpretations. The [Hebrew] Bible is silent on these matters; later literature contains these beliefs, but here, too, there is much difference of opinion." (Ibid 656).

The beliefs that separate Judaism from Christianity are very pronounced. "Judaism's rejection of Christianity is based not only upon its rejection of Jesus as the Messiah, but upon its inability to accept the Pauline elements introduced into Jesus' teachings. These elements are listed by Milton Steinberg in his work *Basic Judaism* as follows: The insistence that the flesh is evil and is to be suppressed; the notion of original sin and damnation from before birth of all human beings; the conception of Jesus not as a man but as God made flesh;

the conviction that men can be saved and that Jesus is God's sacrifice of His only begotten Son so that by believing in him they may be saved;..the final and climactic doctrine that he who earnestly believes these things is automatically saved, but that he who denies them, no matter how virtuous otherwise, is lost." (*Collier's Encyclopedia,* The Crowell-Collier Publishing Co., 1962, Vol. 13, p. 656.)

Does this Jewish view of Christianity give an accurate description of the teachings of the New Testament? That is what this book will attempt to discover. It is one thing to explore the major religions of the world to see what their position is on salvation, but we need to see what an enormous amount of primitive peoples around the world believed about salvation. Almost every group of people in the history of the world, so far as I can ascertain, has, in some way, associated blood with salvation. The study of this connection is the key to understanding the subject of eternal damnation, as written about in the Bible.

H. Clay Trumbull, in *The Blood Covenant,*[1] written more than 100 years ago, gives us the best study I have found on the subject of blood and its significance for mankind and God. Mr. Trumbull spent years in the Middle East during the late 1800's researching the customs of the peoples of the Middle East. He studied and wrote at length about the customs of these people which were unchanged from over two thousand years earlier.

"Beyond the idea of inspiration through an interunion with God by blood. God is life. All life is from God,

----

1. The Blood Covenant, H. Clay Trumbull, Impact Books, Inc. Kirkwood, MO 63122. Quoted with permission.

and belongs to God. Blood is life. Blood therefore, as life, may be a means of man's interunion with God. As the closest and most sacred of covenants between man and man; as, indeed, an absolute merging of two human natures into one,--is a possibility through an inter-flowing of a common blood; so the closest and most sacred of covenants between man and God; so the interunion of the human nature with the divine,--has been looked upon as a possibility, through the proffer and acceptance of a common life in a common blood-flow."

"Whatever has been man's view of sin and its punishment, and of his separation from God because of unforgiven sin (I speak now of man as he is found, without the specific teachings of the Bible on this subject,) he has counted blood--his own blood, in actuality or by substitute--a means of interunion with God, or with the gods. Blood is not death, but life. The shedding of blood, Godward, is not the taking of life, but the giving of life. The outflowing of blood toward God is an act of gratitude or of affection, a proof of loving confidence, a means of inter-union. This seems to have been the universal primitive conception of the [human] race. And an evidence of man's trust in the accomplished fact of his interunion with God, or with the gods, by blood, has been the also universal practice of man's inter-communion with God, or with the gods, by his sharing, in food-partaking, of the body of the sacrificial offering, whose blood is the means of the divine-human interunion." (*The Blood Covenant,* p. 147-148.)

"...in all religions the longing...to enter into the closest possible union with the adored being, is fundamental. This longing is inseparable from the religious sentiment itself, and becomes imperious wherever that sentiment is warm; and this consideration is enough to convince us that it is in harmony with the most exalted tendencies of our nature, but may likewise, in times of ignorance, give rise to the most deplorable aberrations."

(*The Blood Covenant,* p. 183.)

"Man longed for oneness of life with God. Oneness of life could come only through oneness of blood. To secure such oneness of life, man would give of his own blood, or that substitute blood which could best represent himself. Counting himself in oneness of life with God, through the covenant of blood, man has sought for nourishment and growth through partaking of that food which stood for God. In misdirected pursuance of this thought, men have given the blood of a consecrated human victim to bring themselves into union with God; and then they have eaten of the flesh of that victim which had supplied the blood which made them one with God. This seems to be the basis of fact in the premises; whatever may be the understood philosophy of the facts. Why men reasoned thus, may indeed be in question. That they reasoned thus, seems evident." (*The Blood Covenant,* p. 184-185.)

Now, that we have looked at some historical teachings on the subject of eternal damnation, I want to look at the teachings of several varied Christian denominations to see what they say about the subject. I will use the book, *Handbook Of Denominations,* by Frank Mead and Samuel Hill, Abingdon Press, 1985.

ADVENTISM "holds that the nature of the human race is fallen because of sin and that on the basis of neglect or rejection of God's plan of salvation, those rebellious against the government of God will be ultimately destroyed, while believers, by God's grace, will be saved. (p. 19)

The AMERICAN BAPTIST ASSOC. believes "there is eternal punishment for the wicked; salvation is solely by grace through faith and not by law or works. (p. 38)

The FREEWILL BAPTISTS, believe that Christ gave himself a ransom for all, not just the elect; that God calls all of us to repentance; and that whosoever will, may be saved." (p. 47) Another Baptist group has similar views. "The saved are in everlasting felicity; the lost are consigned to endless punishment." (p. 48)

CHRISTIAN CHURCHES and CHURCH OF CHRIST "stress the divinity of Christ, the agency of the Holy Spirit in conversion, the Bible as the inspired Word of God, future rewards and punishments, and God as a prayer-answering deity." (p. 77)

CHURCH OF CHRIST, SCIENTIST, Scientists say, "God forgives sin through destroying it with 'the spiritual understanding that casts out evil as unreal.' The punishment for sin, however lasts as long as the belief in sin endures." (p. 81)

The CHURCH OF GOD of Anderson, Indiana teaches that "the forgiveness of sin through the atonement of Christ and repentance of the believer; the experience of holiness; the personal return of Christ, not connected with any millennial reign; the kingdom of God as established here and now; final judgment; resurrection of the dead; reward of the righteous and punishment of the wicked." (p. 85)

The CHURCHES OF CHRIST, so prevalent in the Southwest of the U.S., while not a denomination, are a group of churches that act more like a denomination than a lot of denominations. "The great scriptural doctrines...the universality of sin after the age of accountability, its only remedy in the vicarious atonement of the Lord Jesus Christ...and baptism by immersion into Christ for the remission of sins." (p. 94)

The FOURSQUARE CHURCHES -- founded by Aimee Semple McPherson -- believe "the usual doctrines on the atonement, the second coming of Christ 'in clouds of glory,' reward for the righteous at the judgment, and eternal punishment for the wicked." (p. 115)

The MORMONS, not exactly a Christian denomination, teach that "persons will be punished for their own individual sins, not for Adam's transgression. All humankind may be saved through the atonement of Christ and by obedience to the laws and ordinances of the gospel; these laws and ordinances include faith in Christ, repentance, baptism by immersion for the remission of sins, the laying on of hands for the gift of the Holy Ghost, and the observance of the Lord's Supper each Sunday." (p. 135)

The METHODISTS teach and preach "the doctrines of the Trinity, the natural sinfulness of humankind, its fall and the need of conversion and repentance, freedom of the will, justification by faith, sanctification and holiness, future rewards and punishments, the sufficiency of the Scriptures for salvation, the enabling grace of God, and perfection." (p. 163)

The ORTHODOX Church, which separated from the Roman Catholic Church says that both faith and works are necessary for justification. "Purgatory is denied, but the dead are prayed for; and it is believed that the dead pray for those on earth." (p. 185) The ORTHODOX Church's centuries old adversary,

the ROMAN CATHOLIC Church, believes that the forgiveness of sins comes by way of baptism. However, any sins committed after baptism can only be forgiven after the sacrament of penance. (p. 225)

The positions of several of the major denominations will be touched on later in this book. By using these few examples of different churches' doctrines, I want to show the varied teachings on what the Bible says about eternal damnation. It is not the objective of this book to give a history of the idea of eternal damnation, but rather, to point out what the Bible says about the subject. I still want to touch a few more points from history to show the mind-set of different peoples.

To look at this subject from a different angle, I will take a few excerpts from the book, *Beyond Death's Door..,*" by Maurice Rawlings, MD., Nelson Publishers, Nashville, TN. The Egyptians around 2500 BC "considered death as just an interruption of life, not its end." (p. 48-49) The Orientals of the far east, according to the Tibetan Book of the Dead, believed that, "in this new state of the released soul, his senses are sharpened and intensified, and he may encounter other spiritual beings, or he may meet a 'clear light' that creates feelings of immense peace and contentment. However, he is eventually judged and sentenced based on his deeds during his physical existence." (p. 48-49)

The Babylonians "believed in the resurrection of the dead, including judgment and punishment. The Persians believed that the soul was struggled for by the 'spirits of good and evil.' If the evil forces won, "he fell into the abyss of the 'house of hell.'" (p. 49) The Greeks had varying beliefs on life after death. Plato taught that each soul had to face the 'judgment,' at which "time all things he had done in his past life were displayed before him." Plato, in the Republic, relates the story of a Greek soldier who had died and lived to tell of a difference between heaven and hell. (p. 50)

The following excerpts are from the same book. The first story is told by Thomas Welch. "I was dead as far as this world is concerned. But I was alive in another world...The next thing I knew I was standing near a shoreline of an ocean of fire. It happened to be what the Bible says it is, in Revelation 21:8:...'the lake which burneth with fire and brimstone.' This is the most awesome sight one could ever see this side of the final judgment" (p. 103)

Another lady related that "the next thing I remember was entering this gloomy room where I saw in one of the windows this huge giant with a grotesque face that was watching me. Running around the windowsill were little imps, or elves, that seemed to be with the giant. The giant beckoned me to come with him. I didn't want to go, but I had to. Outside was darkness but I could hear people moaning all around me. I could feel things moving about my feet. As we moved on through this tunnel or cave, things were getting worse. Then, for some reason, the giant turned me loose and sent me back." (p. 106)   Also, Dr. Rawlings relates Kenneth Hagin's experience, which this author has heard in person sometime in 1982-83. In Hagin's pamphlet, "My Testimony," he recounts his trip to hell, when he died due to illness. I may not agree with him on all points of theology, but I have no reason to question the fact that he had an out-of-body experience and traveled down to hell, only to be rescued by the voice of God.

There is no reason to question the insurmountable evidence, given by people who have had an out-of-body experience, that there is an existence in the spiritual realm that could be considered "hell." To question that would make such persons liars! However, to say that the "hell" that exists in the spirit realm proves a certain theology is ludicrous and would also make a person a liar! Any Christian, or non-Christian, group whose teachings on hell correlate with the out-of-body experiences could say that it proves their theology correct. It does not prove anything of the kind! As I showed earlier, most every religion and denomination had a belief in "hell," each one similar, but not exactly the same. Just because "hell" is a fact does not prove how a person's spirit is, or is not, sent there.

To demonstrate this, I will relate this story. While watching the 700 Club, September 28, 1988, I saw the ridiculousness of this type of logic. They were asking people if they believed in "hell," with most responses they showed being in the negative. What the correspondent, Cynthia Glaser, was trying to point out was that the doctrine of "hell" has lost its impact with people today. She kept stressing a certain doctrine of "hell" that she must have considered the only accepted doctrine on the subject. She never did say exactly what that accepted doctrine is, even though she alluded to God having to punish the sinner for his sin. In her interview of author Roberts Liardon, it became obvious what problem she and most of Christianity has with this subject of "hell." Mr. Liardon stated, "There is a God! There is a heaven! There is a hell! There is a devil! Bamm!! If you don't like it, that's your problem! It's still true!"

The fallacy in all this is that they expect everyone to believe what they believe about God, heaven, hell, and the devil. If you do not believe the same way that they do about these four subjects, it makes you wrong. They are saying that if you do not believe what they do about God, heaven, hell, and the devil, then you are bound for eternal damnation. Hopefully, you can see the ridiculousness of their position and see how this only brings division and denominationalism.

With this book I hope to show you a different way to look at, and believe, that there is a God, a heaven, a hell, and a devil. I am not going to attempt to say that these four subjects do not exist, but we need to start looking at them the way the Bible does. We have seen what some other religions and primitive people have to say about God, heaven, and eternal damnation. However, it may not matter what any other person, or group, has to say about the subject. What we need to decide at this time is: ARE WE GOING TO BELIEVE WHAT THE BIBLE SAYS, OR ARE WE GOING TO GO BY

WHAT PEOPLE TELL US THE BIBLE SAYS? This is going to be one of the most important decisions we will ever make, because, if the Bible is the "Word of God," then He meant for us to believe what *it* says. The reason I am stressing this point at this time is because the rest of this book, will, for most of you, probably question most everything you were ever taught about God, heaven, and hell. If the Bible is going to be our basis of belief, then we need to first, find out what it says, and second, adjust our theology accordingly. As for me, and my house, we are going to believe the truth, and that truth is found in the Bible.

2

A GOD OF LOVE OR WRATH?

The God of the Bible is described as having certain attributes that should reflect His relationship with mankind. It is fairly easy to read through the Bible and find verses that speak of God as having attributes, or characteristics, similar to the characteristics we humans have. There is nothing wrong with this approach to attempting to understand the Creator of the universe because, as we will see later, God created mankind from His own blood (spirit). However, if we determine the characteristics of God and accept them as accurate, so far as human understanding is concerned, then we must thereafter interpret the Bible in line with these attributes.

One of the major problems with Bible interpretation has been that the attributes of God have been determined from the person's interpretation of the Bible; instead of the interpretation of the Bible being determined by understanding the attributes of God.

This can be demonstrated by the following analogy. Throughout the history of the Bible, people have read the Old Testament which showed God as an angry, vengeful God. Then when reading the remainder of the Bible they have this image in mind. However, had they known that one of the main attributes of God is that He is faithful to His Word, meaning He is a covenant-keeping God, they would have seen that His "negative" attributes were always connected with a covenant. Never once was God angry, vengeful, or jealous without previously being obligated to a covenant, therefore necessitating or allowing God to be angry.

This is just one of many analogies that points out the problem with having the wrong basis from which to interpret the Bible. The same thing is true when studying the subject of eternal damnation. People read how God, in the Old Testament, obliterated His opponents, or non-believers, and just assume that He must be the same way with opponents and unbelievers in the New Testament. This is the typical way that people have interpreted the Bible. However, it may not be the way the Bible should be interpreted.

God has attributes similar to some attributes possessed by humans. But God's attributes are more magnified when compared to ours. More magnified in the sense that when we talk about love for us, for God it is "*agape,*" which is a level of love that is difficult for humans to comprehend. Also, when we speak of keeping our word, what we are really saying is that almost always we will stand behind what we say. When God says He is faithful, a covenant-keeping God, He really means that *never, never, ever* will He not stand behind His Word!

I have already mentioned one of the most often forgotten attributes of God, that being the fact that He is a covenant-keeping God. "...O Lord, great and awesome God, who keeps His covenant and mercy with those who love Him, and with those who keep His commandments." (Daniel 9:4) "Therefore know that the Lord your God, He is God, the faithful God who keeps covenant and mercy for a thousand generations with those who love and keep His commandments; and He repays those who hate Him to their face, to destroy them. He will not be slack with him who hates Him; He will repay him to his face." (Deuteronomy 7:9-10)

Before explaining why God appears to be so vengeful, let us look at Exodus 34:6-7. "And the Lord passed before him (Moses) and proclaimed, 'The Lord, the Lord God, merciful and gracious, long-suffering, and abounding in goodness and truth, keeping mercy for thousands, forgiving iniquity and transgression of sins, by no means clearing the guilty, visiting the iniquity of the fathers upon the children and the children's children to the third and fourth generation."

God appears very vengeful in these verses because, not only is He a God who insures the blessings of the covenant, when the other party obeys the covenant, but also He insures that the curse of the covenant will come upon the offender if the covenant is not obeyed. When God keeps covenant, He insures all of it, both the positive and negative.

Another way of looking at God's faithfulness is Romans 3:3, which speaks of the Jews who had broken covenant. "For what if some did not believe? Will their unbelief make the faithfulness of God without effect?" Just because a person refuses to believe, or is unable to believe, how does that effect God's faithfulness? According to this verse, a person's lack of belief in a covenant does not affect God's belief in that same covenant. Now, taking this piece of knowledge about one of God's main attributes and applying it to our Bible interpretation, will it necessitate a change?

One more of God's attributes that has been neglected is that God is impartial. "For there is no partiality with God." (Romans 2:11) "And you, masters, do the same things to them, giving up threatenings, knowing that your own Master also is in heaven, and there is no partiality with Him." (Ephesians 6:9) "Then Peter opened his mouth and said; 'In truth I perceive that God shows no partiality." (Acts 10:34) "For the Lord your God is God of gods and Lord of lords, the great God, mighty and awesome, who shows no partiality nor takes a bribe." (Deuteronomy 10:17)

In order to get a clear picture of God's impartiality we need a definition. Impartiality means that, if there is anything that affects everyone, when the very same rules must apply to everyone. No exceptions! For instance, if salvation, or eternal damnation, or baptism affects everyone, then the same rules must apply equally to everyone. If even one person is under even one different rule, then partiality has been shown to one category or the other. Therefore, we must determine what parts of the Bible apply to everyone and base our interpretation on the fact that God treats us all the same.

But, "What about all the verses that talk about God's chosen people, God hardening their hearts, God exalting this person or that person?" Keep in mind the definition. If the situation does not affect everyone, then He is not obligated to have the same rules.

Let me use an analogy from umpiring baseball. The pitcher, while pitching, is subject to different rules than the catcher. An umpire cannot call a balk on the catcher, but the umpire can call a balk on the pitcher. However, when either the catcher, or the pitcher, becomes a batter, or base runner, each one is subject to the same rules. Each player is still the pitcher or catcher, but something else has come into play. The same principle applies to God's relationship with mankind. When a person from God's "chosen group", and a person from God's "hated" group, are confronted with the same situation, then God must apply the same rule(s) to each person. If He does not, then He is not impartial, and the Bible is a lie.

Probably the most familiar of God's characteristics is that God is love (Greek-*agape*). The meaning of this word is, for the most part, lost on our Western Culture. The love that the word *agape* denotes is such a deep love, that probably few of us have ever seen it. It is so unlike the love we see every day that we have trouble fathoming the love that God has for us. When the New Testament talks about God loving mankind it always uses the word *agape, agapao,* or *phileo.* (The latter word is used sometimes when involving a covenant relationship.) This Greek word *agape,* from my research, can best be defined as a serving love, of being a servant to those whom you are to be loving. The magnitude of this definition brings about the conclusion that this love is seldom seen in mankind. That is understandable, considering that we allow ourselves to be so programmed with the love that we see around us that asks, "What is in this for me?" We have to admit it. No matter how much we love our friends or family, we all still have those moments when selfishness creeps in to control the relationship.

With God *(agape)*, selfishness is not found. God is always serving. Serving is done from a subordinate position, and most people cannot picture the Creator of this universe in a subordinate position. But, it is a loving subordinate position, much like a wife/mother who serves her family not because she has to, but because of her love for her family.

We have to keep in mind that God created "from one blood every nation of men..." (Acts 17:26), and that blood came from God himself. He put into mankind His own blood (spirit), so that we have to look at each person as having God's blood in them, and we must base our interpretation of the Bible on that historical fact.

This fact also gives us the insight we need to understand God's love *(agape)* toward mankind. When we understand that we are his actual children, we can then get a much clearer picture of His relationship with mankind by comparing it with our human parent-child relationship. Imagine the best parent-child relationship you can hope to have. Then imagine how this human relationship might compare with a parent-child relationship where the parent is the Creator of this universe.

If we do not look at how strong this tie is between God and mankind, whether believer or unbeliever, we may end up being confused about where people end up after they die. We must honestly question the teaching that God is going to punish this child, or that child, for eternity, because they did not accept His love. Would we do the same? Ask yourself this question: What could my child do to me, or anyone else that would make me separate myself from them for eternity? Now, how do you think God, who loves us more than we love our own children, would answer that question?

One other attribute of God that is important to our discussion of this subject is that God can do what He wants to do, whenever He wants to do it. Most people call this sovereignty. He is limited by Himself only if He decides to limit Himself. If it is true that God possesses this attribute, then we need to find out if God put limits on Himself, and if He did, what are those limits?

For the purposes of limiting our discussion of this subject at this time, suffice it to say that God limited Himself by agreeing to covenants with mankind. This is evident throughout the Bible, therefore making it common knowledge. If we find that God is faithful to His Word, then we know that God relinquished some of His sovereignty when He agreed to these covenants. The reason we need to understand this is so that we can reprogram ourselves away from the idea that we never know what God will do, because He is sovereign, and therefore we are subject to His every whim and fancy.

Knowing that God has limited Himself leaves us obligated to learn exactly how he has limited Himself. The result of this will be freedom from ignorance and fear of the unknown. Knowledge brings freedom in the secular world. The same is true when it comes to Bible subjects, and that is what we will find in studying the subject of eternal damnation.

Mankind has been so programmed with the idea that all rulers, kings, leaders, or gods could do whatever they wanted to do, whenever they wanted to do it, that this thought has also been transferred to God. Studying history will reinforce this premise. Until the United States government was formed, there had seldom been limits put on leadership. Leaders could change rules when it was in their best interest to do so. If all we see is authoritarianism, it is difficult for us to fathom a God who rules by serving, or a God who makes agreements with man and then sticks to those agreements, even to the point of putting His entire creation in a trust with a third party, which we will see later.

These are the attributes of God that must be kept in mind while reading the rest of this book. God's greatest attribute is that, He is *agape*, and we need to keep that foremost in our minds when reading the Bible. We must also be mindful of the fact that He is a faithful, covenant-keeping God who must, and will, treat everyone equally within His love. The impartiality of God is probably the least recognized, and understood, attribute of God. We will find out later how this is true.

3

KINGDOM OF HEAVEN, OR

REALM OF HEAVEN?

We need to find out why Christians have confused
these terms "Kingdom of Heaven" and "Heaven." Basically, the reason we have done that is that we have just
assumed that the two terms have referred to the "Realm
of Heaven" rather than the Kingdom of Heaven, which
are two distinctly different categories. The realm of
Heaven is in the spirit realm. The Kingdom of Heaven is
anything ruled by Heaven. The best book that I came
across for explaining what the writers of the Gospels
understood about the concepts of "Kingdom of Heaven"
and the "Kingdom of God," is the book, *Jesus, Rabbi
And Lord*, by Robert L. Lindsey.

Dr. Lindsey points out certain reasons for the use of
the term "Kingdom of Heaven". "....the rabbis often
talked about 'the Kingdom of Heaven,' by which they
meant 'the Kingdom of God.' They were afraid of trans-
gressing the command not to 'take the name of the Lord
in vain.' So, as was their habit, they said that if the actual
name of the Lord is not said, you cannot transgress this
commandment at all: use some evasive synonym and you
will not break this law. The expression in Hebrew is
molchut chanimajim, Kingdom of Heaven, Heaven being
an evasive synonym for God.

"This phrase, of course, as "Kingdom of Heaven"

37

was apparently developed by the sect of Jews called the Pharisees. It is not used in the Dead Sea scrolls. In essence they meant that any Jew who would seriously follow the Torah [the Law] had accepted the Lordship of God, that is, prepared to do whatever the Law demanded of him. They did not mean by *molchut chanimajim*, as so many Christians have supposed, some kind of future political supremacy by which the Messiah and Israel would rule the earth from Jerusalem. They, of course, believed that God rules the whole earth. But when they used this special expression "Kingdom of Heaven," they did not mean God's general rule of the whole world, they meant that any Jew who began to keep the Torah and the rabbinic interpretations of the Torah had come under the rule of the Law and was now in God's rule or kingdom. He had taken upon himself "the yoke of the Kingdom of God" or simply, "the Kingdom of God." [p24]

There is a second meaning behind the concept of the "Kingdom of God," Jesus borrowed the term from the Pharisees and gave that name to His movement. Movement?! What movement did Jesus have going? This is an area where Christianity has made a big blunder by not understanding this concept.

"By inviting followers to call Him Lord and to itinerate with Him in Galilee and Judea, Jesus organized a Movement which he saw as made up of those he called disciples and which he called "the Kingdom of God."

"In rabbinic sources we hear often of famous rabbis who gathered *talmidim,* learners, around them and taught them Torah and rabbinic traditions about the Torah. The difference seems to be that Jesus not only called *talmidim* to learn Torah from him, but also, eventually to be granted powers of healing and exorcism in His name so that they could perform the same kinds of miracles He performed." [p 53]

"...and it was from this band of itinerating followers who go with Him from place to place that He afterwards chooses twelve to be His *shelichim*, or apostles. It was, of course, this latter group of specially chosen leaders who eventually headed and guided the movement Jesus founded." [p 54]

"...Jesus was forming a band of followers who were prepared not only to learn from Him, but to carry out any requirement of life or duty He laid upon them. These are the people in our Gospels who call Jesus 'Lord!' When they join His learners, he says they have 'come unto' or 'received' the Kingdom of Heaven, that is the Kingdom of God.

"The Kingdom of God is the place where God is reigning, or if you wish, the person or community he is ruling. Jesus, explains that when He casts out a demon 'the Kingdom of God' has come upon all those present, that is, God has taken charge of a situation in which formerly the devil ruled. God has penetrated the very spot in which men find themselves under Satan's control." [p 55]

"Let me say it again: for Jesus the Kingdom of God is not some spacious, grandiose way of talking about how God is ruling the entire world controlling kings and empires and allowing or preventing national and international disasters, but is strictly, in this second sense, a term used to designate those who are in the Jesus movement." [p 59]

The real problem with this subject is that Christians have just assumed that the term "heaven," meant the realm of heaven in the spiritual realm, rather than realizing that when the word, "kingdom," goes with it, it means to be ruled by Heaven. What we need to do is take a look at these verses in the New Testament to find out how the terms are used. They talk about the Kingdom of Heaven and we will see what is meant.

"In those days John the Baptist came preaching in the wilderness of Judea and saying, "Repent for the Kingdom of Heaven is at hand!" (Matthew 3:1) We see that John is saying that the Kingdom of Heaven is at hand, not that the realm of Heaven is at hand. God's rulership is at hand, meaning Jesus was about to appear.

"From that time Jesus began to preach and to say, 'Repent for the Kingdom of Heaven is at hand.'" Here again we see that Jesus said the same thing. Repent for the Kingdom of Heaven is at hand. The people were soon to have access to the Kingdom of Heaven and Jesus in this verse was telling the people to change their thinking (repent).

"Now Jesus went about all Galilee teaching in their synagogues, preaching the gospel of the kingdom, and healing all kinds of sickness and all kinds of disease among the people." (Matthew 4:23) It appears to be the same kingdom, even if they did not use the term Kingdom of Heaven.

The interesting thing here is the use of the term "the gospel." Was He speaking of the same gospel that He told the disciples to preach? Or, possibly the same gospel that God preached before to Abraham? Or was it the "gospel" that is preached by evangelical Christians today?

If it was the same gospel of evangelical Christianity, then we can assume that he was telling them to repent, or go to hell. After all, that is the gospel according to most of Christianity. They tell people to repent, if they do not want to spend eternity in hell. [It is hard to argue against this being the accepted gospel of Christianity.]

But, that is not the same gospel that Jesus wanted these people to believe in. What He was trying to get these people to believe in, was the Abrahamic covenant which they could receive the blessings of, if they would only believe in that covenant, since it was the only covenant in force, of which they could be a part. That this covenant is the gospel of which Jesus spoke, is quite obvious. Also, obvious, is the lack of reference to eternal damnation or the realm of heaven.

We have to remember that God had preached the covenant (gospel) to Abraham, (Galatians 3:8). Then, here we see Jesus telling people to believe in the gospel, which could only refer to the Abrahamic Covenant, because it was the only option these Jews had to rise above their misery.

Anytime the Jews had been blessed, it was directly related to their obedience to a covenant. So, this period of time in which Jesus lived was no different. The people were in misery because they had not obeyed the covenant. They were living under the curse of the covenant, and all that Jesus wanted them to do was turn it around, to believe in the blessings of the covenant, and obey the laws of the covenant.

We have to understand this connection between gospel and covenant. This is one of the main reasons Christians have missed the teaching on eternal damnation. We have separated gospel and covenant, refusing to keep our preaching of the gospel consistent with the rest of the Bible. If both God and His Son, Jesus, preached the covenant, then maybe we should also.

In Mark 16:15, we see the first words of Christianity's Great Commission. This section of the Bible, questioned by most Bible scholars, is where many Christians get their inspiration to go tell the world to repent. The verse says to, "Go into all the world and preach the gospel to every creature. He who believes and is baptized will be saved; but he who does not believe will be condemned." (Mark 16:15-16)

It is obvious to see by reading these verses why Christians have thought the gospel was to be preached with damnation as a consequence of unbelief. However, we know this to be incorrect, not only because this section of Mark 16 was not in the early manuscripts, but also because it does not hold true, when put up against the definition of gospel. Not only that, but it does not stay consistent with justification, redemption, reconciliation, atonement, and the eternal Covenant, etc.

For some people, the exclusion of this section from the older manuscripts would be proof enough for them to write off this, so called, "Great Commission" as inaccurate and not God's Word. But, for me, since I am not a great Bible scholar, I find it easier to divide the Word of Truth by consistent interpretation. If the Bible contains the Word of God, then it will certainly be consistent. Anything not consistent, is obviously not from God.

This leaves us looking for inconsistencies that we can throw out, and consistencies which we can believe and act on. Which is how we can conclude that the gospel that Jesus wants us to preach is the covenant. The only thing we have to figure out now is: "Which covenant?" We find that out in another chapter of this book.

What we needed to clear up in this chapter is the difference between the Kingdom of Heaven and the Realm of Heaven. We are a part of the Kingdom of Heaven, but we are not in the Realm of Heaven. The Kingdom of Heaven is anything ruled by God, whereas the Realm of Heaven is in the spirit world, or dimension, which we cannot see with our natural eyes, because its molecules move at a faster rate of speed than the physical realm.

This differentiation of terms must be made to get a correct interpretation of what the Bible writers were trying to get across. To get into the Kingdom of Heaven, we need to be born-again, where we turn over rulership of our life to Jesus. To get into the Realm of Heaven, we do not have to do anything, except die. We cannot get in any other way. The Kingdom of Heaven is now! It always has been, and always will be. The Realm of Heaven can be accessed by us in the name of Jesus, but we do not "reside" there until death.

"Your kingdom come. Your will be done on earth as it is in heaven." We have all repeated this prayer many, many times, but has it really become real to us. Instead of waiting to be taken out of this physical existence, maybe we should be about the business of helping to establish God's Kingdom on the earth. By preaching a "heaven, or damnation gospel," the emphasis is on populating the realm of Heaven instead of the Kingdom of Heaven.

"Seek first the Kingdom of Heaven, and all these (physical) things will be added to you." We have all heard this verse many, many times, but have we realized that it was telling us to seek the rulership of Heaven, not the realm of Heaven? Allowing God to rule in every area of our life opens the way for the blessings of God to get to us. The blessings of God are always there. We are the ones that stop the flow, which is one of the most important points to know about the teachings on this subject.

4

BAPTISM SHOULD IT BE WET OR DRY?

Baptism is probably the most divisive doctrine of Christianity. Practically every denomination has some type of ritual they call baptism. Some denominations say that you are not a Christian until you are baptized in, or with water. It is just amazing how many different interpretations stem from a subject that is very simple when it comes to what the Bible says.

Reading through the Old Covenant, we can see the ceremonial washings, which were a form of baptism. Also, we have to keep in mind that almost all of the four gospels of the New Testament are still in a period of time when the Jews were still functioning under the Old Covenant. It was not until Jesus died that the New Covenant came into force. Therefore, those people in the gospels, were functioning under laws that no longer pertain to us at this time. That is probably the most important thing we must realize about this teaching of baptism.

Jesus was baptized by John the Baptist under Old Covenant instructions. What actually happened was that John was up on the bank of the river. Each person wanting to be baptized would go into the water by themselves. Nobody would touch them. These were ceremonial washings, or baptisms. The ceremonial cleansings were usually performed in the ritual immersion baths. The reason for this ceremony of baptism was for atonement, or for the forgiveness of sins.[1]

The baptism of the Jewish proselyte was important to Judaism, as was circumcision, and sacrifice. The baptism was performed in the presence of three witnesses, ordinarily Sanhedaranists. The person to be baptized, having cut his hair and nails, undressed completely, made a fresh profession of his faith, before what were designated the fathers of the baptism, and were then immersed completely, so that every part of his body was touched by water.

The rite would, of course, be accompanied by exhortations and benedictions. Baptism was not to be administered at night, nor on a Sabbath or a feast day... Women were attended by those of their own sex, with the Rabbis standing at the door outside.

The waters of baptism were to him, in very proof, though very far from the Christian sense, the basis of regeneration. As he stepped out of these waters, he was considered as born anew. In the language of the Rabbis, as if he were a little child just born. More especially, he was to regard himself as a new man in reference to his past; country, home, habits, friends, and relations were all changed. The past, with all that had belonged to it, was past. He was a new man. The old, with its defilement was buried in the waters of baptism.

This is the background of the ceremony that Jesus and John the Baptist performed. But what we have not realized is that we have blindly clung to this idea that Jesus was baptized, so therefore, we must be baptized. That could not be further from the truth. Just because

----

1. I obtained my information for this section from a recognized Hebrew scholar who did not wish to be quoted.

Jesus did something does not mean we have to do the same thing.

Jesus was following the ceremonial washings of the Old Covenant. He was not doing or saying anything wrong under that covenant. When He told John that they must fulfill all righteousness, He was doing this according to rules that do not apply to us, living since His death. He fulfilled all righteousness according to the rules he agreed to obey. Are we required to do the same? Maybe yes, maybe no.

Now, we want to go through the New Testament and find out exactly what the writers had to say about baptism. First let's refer back to the idea of the Old Covenant and the New Covenant. Matthew 20:22 says, "But Jesus answered and said, 'You do not know what you ask. Are you able to drink the cup that I am about to drink, and be baptized with the baptism that I am baptized with?' They said to Him, "We are able."

What did Jesus reply? He said that they would be baptized with the baptism that He was baptized with. That is not saying that it was water baptism, because, being religious men, in all likelihood, they had already gone through the ceremony of water baptism, therefore wiping it out as a possibility.

Here we have the baptism He was baptized with, and the people He was talking to, His disciples, were going to have the same baptism. It does not say that it was going to be before, or after, the new covenant came into force.

A few verses in Acts talk about all the believers being added to the church, and how they were baptized the very same day [Acts 2:41, 8:12, 16:33]. Well, there is no problem with that. So what if they were? It does not say they were baptized in water, does it? They could have been, but we really do not know for sure. With the ceremonial baths that were available there in Jerusalem, there would not have been any problem with baptizing that many people in one day. Then again, I am not saying that is the way they were baptized. Even if the early church observed this ceremony, does not mean it is a commandment of God for everyone.

"Or do you not know that as many of us as were baptized into Christ Jesus were baptized into His death? Therefore we were buried with Him through baptism into death, that just as Christ was raised from the dead by the glory of the Father, even so we also should walk in newness of life." (Romans 6:3-4) It says that we were baptized into Christ Jesus and in doing that were baptized into His death. How are we baptized into Jesus?

Verse 4 says that we are buried with Him through baptism into death. Through baptism? Now, how are we buried into Christ Jesus, into His death, through baptism? Certainly not water baptism. That is ridiculous! There is nothing in the history of the world that correlates with that idea, other than a few small groups like the Hebrews who believed that water baptism brought about a born-again experience. Later, some Christians accepted this same false teaching.

The idea of water baptism causing a person to become a new person, does not line up with the beliefs of the rest of the world. The rest of the entire world knew that a person could only be born again by making a blood covenant with another person. This understanding, as we have learned from the study of blood covenants, was prevalent in all parts of the world throughout history. Will we be able to prove this by studying the New Testament?

"Moreover brother, I do not want you to be unaware that all our fathers were under the cloud, all passed through the sea, all were baptized into Moses as in the cloud and in the sea, all ate the same spiritual food, and all drank the same spiritual drink for they drank of that spiritual rock that followed them and that rock was Christ." (I Corinthians 10:1-4) We see here that all those people were baptized into Moses in the cloud and in the sea.

Now, how did they get baptized into Moses? In Romans 6:3-4, we saw that a person could be baptized into Christ Jesus, and now we see that a person could be baptized into Moses. None of these verses say anything about water. They just talk about baptism.

The Greek word "*baptismo*" means, "immersion," but it still does not suggest water immersion. Also, in I Corinthians 12:13 we see this idea. "For by one spirit we were all baptized into one body--whether Jews or Greeks, whether slaves or free--and have all been made to drink into one spirit." Here it says we are all baptized into one body.

You will notice that the baptism spoken of here, "being baptized into one body," is accomplished not by water, but by a [one] spirit. This is consistent with the principles of covenanting whereby the rebirth takes place by the transference of blood [spirit]. This verse, by itself, disproves the water baptism theology, and proves the validity of the use of covenant principles for correct Bible interpretation.

Moving on, we see in Colossians 3:27, "For as many of you as were baptized into Christ have put on Christ." We see again that we are baptized *into* Christ. Was it by water? Not at all. The only way to get into someone is by making a blood covenant with them. Also, in verse 28 we see this again. "There is neither Jew nor Greek, there is neither slave or free, there is neither male nor female, for you are one in Christ Jesus."

This goes along with I Corinthians 12:13, about neither Jew nor Greek, nor male or female, because you are all baptized into Christ.

Ephesians 4:1-6 says, "I, therefore, the prisoner of the Lord, beseech you to have a walk worthy of the calling with which you were called, with all lowliness and gentleness, with long suffering, bearing with one another in love, endeavoring to keep the unity of the Spirit in a bond of peace. There is one body and one spirit, just as you were called in the hope of your calling; one Lord, one faith, one baptism: one God and Father of all, who is above all, and through all, and in you all." Here it says there is one Lord, one faith, and one baptism.

I find it amazing that Christians have decided that this "one baptism" is a baptism in water. But, it does not say that at all. Remember what John the Baptist said in Matthew 3:11, "I indeed baptize you with water unto repentance, but he who is coming after me is mightier than I, whose sandals I am not worthy to carry. He will baptize you with the Holy Spirit and fire." This "*He will baptize you with the Holy Spirit and fire,*" would that be the *one* baptism?

It says nothing about water baptism, and if John is talking about a time when the New Covenant would come into force, and, remembering covenant principles, under a different covenant you have different laws, then we can conclude that the laws from the old covenant with the ceremonial washings, the baptisms, would not necessarily, and probably not, come into use under the new covenant. Therefore, logically speaking, the baptism that John the Baptist is talking about here is with the Holy Spirit and with fire. This may not be the only conclusion.

We can prove this conclusion wrong just by looking at a few verses that talk about being baptized into Jesus.

Being baptized with the Holy Spirit and with fire, according to what Jesus said about sending, or giving the Holy Spirit as comforter, teacher, etc., is a different baptism than the baptism into Jesus.

We can conclude this because it lines up with the historically accurate principles of covenanting. There are two principles: first the covenant is made and next each partner gives the best gift possible to the other partner. This action seals the covenant, which is what Jesus does with us when we accept God's Holy Spirit to live in us.

The historical definition of baptism, when related to covenants, is to be immersed into someone just as the Israelites were immersed into Moses, when Moses mediated the covenant for them. The same is true when we make covenant with, or give our life to, Jesus. At that time, we are baptized into Jesus.

Colossians 2:11-12 says, "In Him you were also circumcised with the circumcision made without hands, by putting off the body of the sins of the flesh, by the circumcision of Christ, buried with Him in baptism, in which you also were raised with Him through faith in the working of God, who raised Him from the dead." It does not say we were raised with Him through faith in the working of God, if we were buried with Him in water baptism. [Most of us were probably raised up by the preacher who pulled us up out of the water.] But, we were buried with Him in baptism by giving Him our life, by being baptized into Jesus.

"There is also an anti-type which now saves us, namely baptism (not the removal of the filth of the flesh, but the answer of a good conscience toward God), through the resurrection of Jesus Christ who has gone into heaven and is at the right hand of God, angels, and authorities, and powers having been made subject to

Him." (I Peter 3:21-22) Verse 21, proves that it is not water baptism that is being spoken of throughout the New Testament. What Peter is talking about is the baptism that is the answer of a good conscience toward God.

How do we get a good conscience? The only way to get a good conscience is to get a new spirit in us. The only way that it can get into us is by making a blood covenant with somebody who has uncorrupted blood (good conscience), which brings us to Jesus.

There is only one baptism needed in Christianity and that is a giving of our life to Jesus, or making a covenant with Jesus. At that time, He is baptized into us and we are baptized into Him. His life comes into us and our life goes into Him.

Another reason there can only be one baptism is that, if it were necessary for us to be baptized in water, then God would have a big problem with being a just and fair God. That is because, not all places on the face of the earth are blessed with an abundance of water in which to baptize people with sprinkling, let alone, with immersion. Follow the logic. Just recently we had the famines in Ethiopia and Somalia which brought the attention of the globe to that area of the world. If any of those people had gotten "saved," it would have taken enormous amounts of water just to baptize these people, in order for them to get to heaven. The authorities would not have allowed water to be used for such a purpose, leaving those people on their way to hell because they could not be baptized.

The logic does not hold true. For God to be a fair, impartial, and just God, the rules must pertain to everyone equally, no matter where they live, and no matter when they live. That is the only way for God to remain true to His attribute of being a just God. When we take into consideration the principles of covenants, and the justice of God, there is no way that anyone could honestly believe that water baptism has anything to do with a person's salvation. It is time that Christians teach the facts of baptism.

Another very important fact about New Covenant baptism is that it lines up with the principles of covenanting. As touched on in another part of this book, when a covenant is made between two parties only those two parties can make demands on the other.

When you give your life to Jesus, you become a new person in Christ Jesus. You then have a right to demand (ask for) the greatest gift He can give to you. What He will do then is give to you (baptize you with) His covenant Partner's Holy Spirit, to live in you, to lead you and guide you. This is the greatest gift He can give. He gives the same gift to all, but the Gift manifests itself differently within each person, which, lines up with Covenant principles. Each person is to be led individually within the parameters of the basic rules governing family, religious community and secular governments.

What this means in relation to New Covenant baptism is that each person will be led to their own individual and personal baptism experience. The idea of mass baptisms, or even individual baptisms led by a preacher or even a John the Baptist is an Old Covenant concept that has stifled the work of the Holy Spirit. It is an awesome experience of freedom when you allow the Holy Spirit to lead you to your own personal baptism experience.

The personal baptism experience can take on many different forms. One woman related how she felt led to fall back into a shallow pool of muddy water out in the woods. When she finally gave into this leading of the Holy Spirit she fell back and came up looking muddy, but feeling clean. Although she had been through a baptismal ceremony at a younger age, she will now point to this as her baptism experience.

What this woman's experience typifies is the individuality of the experience. What it also typifies is how humbling the experience can be. This will probably be the stumbling block for most people when the Holy Spirit is trying to lead them to their personal "immersion pool." What a person will find in their "immersion pool" is certainly not for me to say.

It may be fresh, salt, muddy or bottled water. It may be olive, canola, palm, or motor oil. You may be lead to fill a wash tub with a case of Pepsi, soggy cornflakes, or Jack Daniels. Whatever it is that you are led to immerse yourself into, you know that the experience is unique to you, proving again that the God of the Bible is a personal God.

5

IS IT SIN, OR IS IT PROGRAMING?

While growing up as a Pentecostal preacher's kid, I was well aware of all the "sins" a person could commit. The day we found an opened pack of cigarettes with matches at the tennis courts, I could not help but think I was bound for "hell fire," because I had lit one and put it to my lips. But, then again, I had not inhaled, so maybe I would be okay.

Putting one cigarette to my lips was even worse than the night my brother David and I spent more than five dollars each on pin-ball machines. That was when they were six plays for twenty five cents. We did some serious "sinning" that night.

What I found so confusing even as a child was how God kept changing His mind about what was sin. My older brothers could not play organized baseball on Sunday, but then by the time I was old enough to play for the Little League All Stars, it was okay to play on Sunday. I guess God had changed His mind.

Another category God kept changing His mind about was women's apparel and general appearance. The dresses had to be long, just like the hair. Make-up and jewelry, other than a wedding ring, was a definite no-no. Slacks and shorts? Heresy!! Plain Jane was the commandment! Ugly was the result!

Need I mention that we were forbidden to dance, go to movies, play games of chance, cards, or "keepers" in marbles? "Hell fire" certainly awaited the person who let any form of alcohol pass his or her lips.

Not until I went to college did I learn a couple of cute sayings on the subject of sin. These were given to me by my roommate, Gaylon McElfresh of Pacific, Mo. He said that, "Pentecostals (Christians) did not want you to drink, smoke, or chew, or run around with women that do!" At a later date, while in a philosophical stupor, he exclaimed, "Pentecostals are too worried that somebody, somewhere out there, may be having some fun!"

Also, while in college, I started drinking wine occasionally. What I discovered after a few years was the same as I had discovered after attending movies for several years. What I had thought were guilt feelings for having "sinned" (wine and movies), was actually pro-gramming caused by years of preaching against alcohol and movies. The only guilt was in my head and not in my "soul."

Did you ever make a seemingly stupid statement, then years later found out that it was quite profound? Or, am I the only one? I was guilty of this when asked in a young adult Sunday School class what I thought was sin. My answer that 90% of what was considered sin, was actually programming, was met by scoffing by the others in the class. It wasn't until I became a Bible scholar that I discovered how correct that statement was. In fact, in all my years of study, I never came across an adequate definition of sin, so what I had to do was come up with my own. The only surprise for me was how simple the definition is.

In the most simple terms, whenever people are not serving, they are sinning. This principle always holds true no matter what the circumstances, or the parties involved in each situation. Of course, it also follows that whenever you are serving, then you are not sinning!

Serving is the one characteristic that separates Christianity from all other religions. The most important principle Jesus laid out to His followers is that all leaders of His movement (The Kingdom of Heaven) are to be servants of the ones they are leading.

Matthew 20:25-28 specifically shows the rules of leadership within not only Christianity, but also all of God's creation. "But Jesus called them to Himself and said, 'You know that the rulers of the Gentiles lord it over them, and those who are great exercise authority over them.'"

"Yet it shall not be among you; but whoever desires to become great among you, let him be your servant. And whoever desires to be first among you, let him be your slave - just as the Son of Man did not come to be served, but to serve, and to give his life a ransom for many."

Not only did Jesus set down the rules for His followers, but He also gave us insight into the type of Creator in which His followers believe. Our leader, God the Father, The Creator of this universe, the Giver of Life is a servant to us. This teaching of Jesus is totally contrary to all other religions. No other religion is structured in such a way that the one who is worshiped is the one who serves the worshipers. This is the uniqueness of true Christianity.

Some religions may encourage serving within their respective religious community, but none require that the adherents are always servants, no matter what the situation. Only "true Christianity" requires its members to always serve, no matter what the situation. This clarifies for us the definition of sin. If we are not serving, then we are sinning.

For example, eating a large amount of food can be a sin, but it is not always a sin. A person with a high metabolism may not be sinning when eating a large amount of food. Whereas, a person with a low metabolism would probably be sinning when eating a large amount of food.

The word "sin" in the New Testament means nothing more than "to miss the mark." It comes from a Greek archery term. When they missed the mark, they sinned. Now spiritualize the term and how it applies in God's Kingdom. Think of God's Word as the mark, or the standard. Whenever a person does not attain to that standard, in whatever area of life, they have sinned, or missed the mark. It is not that it makes us a bad person, and it certainly does not bring out God's anger against us.

We need to look at it this way. God has set standards of basic perfection for people to aspire to, what we might call, the bullseye. Achieving anything less than this is sinning, or not hitting the bullseye. You should note that a target has some pretty nice territory surrounding the bullseye, but according to the Greek definition, that would be a sin to hit that area, even though it is not all that bad.

That is how God looks at sin. We may miss the mark, or not attain the highest standard, but it does not mean we are out of the contest. So many people have perceived God as having a standard too high to attain so they do not even try. Not so! If we look really close, we will find those standards we thought were God's were *actually set up by man*. God's yoke is easy and His burden is light.

Christians today are no different than the Pharisees

of Jesus' time. They have made up these religions, traditions, theologies and say they are God's way. But, they are not God's way. Let's take some time to explain how we can spot which doctrines are God's and which ones are not. It is really quite simple. We do not have to fast and pray about it, but we will know instantly if it lines up with God's Word.

Most all religions or denominations have the same basic rules for all members. At some point in their history, all members on the same level, have had to perform the same requirements, or rituals, whether these were salvation rituals, initiation rituals, or just regular obligations required for continued membership.

In some religions, some members moved to different levels than other members, so the requirements may vary on each level. The picture that I want you to see is that everyone of them have certain requirements and obligations which must be performed for membership, or to continue membership.

How do these characteristics line up with the principles of covenanting? They don't! After you get past the basic rules of family government, religious community government, secular society relationships, and basic rules of life, which apply to everyone no matter when they live, then the covenant relationship kicks in and takes precedence over all other factors.

In a covenant relationship, only the parties involved can make requirements of the other party. No one outside the covenant can force requirements or obligations on the parties in the covenant. If we would take this simple little principle, we can use it as a yardstick to see if a certain doctrine measures up to God's way of doing it.

A closer look at this principle, and how it applies in

God's Kingdom is needed. We know that in order for people to come into spirit oneness with God, they must give their life to Jesus, or in other words, make covenant with Jesus. Now, if the principle we are discussing is true, then it follows that in this covenant, whereby a person is born-again, only Jesus is allowed to make requirements. Just as anyone in a covenant with Jesus is allowed to make requirements of Jesus, but they cannot make requirements of anyone else not in this covenant.

Now, this is a fuzzy area for most Christians. We have not separated the covenants. We have run them together, overlapped them, and basically confused a very simple part of God's Kingdom. One of the biggest problems is assuming that just because another person is in a similar covenant relationship, that the same requirements apply.

In the Gospel of John we see a good example of this in the last few verses of that gospel where he writes about Peter's concern for the relationship between Jesus and John. What Peter was doing was no different than denominations today. He was sticking his nose where it did not belong. Jesus flat out told him. "What's it to you?!" In reality, Peter was questioning John's covenant, and he had no business doing that. [John 21:20-25]

Christianity has been overrun by do-gooders following in the steps of Peter. So concerned by what someone else's relationship with Jesus might be, they judge another person's relationship by their own standard. To them, Jesus says, "What's it to you?!" Jesus is the one who sets the standard, and He will determine if a person is measuring up to His standard.

Another problem we have in this area is reading, for example, Paul's writings, and saying that everything he said applies to us today. That could not be further from the truth because it violates the principle of covenanting.

Paul has no business telling us what requirements we have in our relationship with Jesus. Actually, we have no business allowing Paul to tell us the requirements of our covenant. The problem, in a nutshell, is studying Paul more than we fellowship with God through His Holy Spirit.

We have to see this principle and how it applies to us, each Christian individually. What does Christianity think God's Holy Spirit was given for? He did not just need a place to hang out! He wanted to lead and guide us into all truth. Is that not what Jesus said? "If I go away I will send the Comforter, and He will lead you into all truth" [John 16:7-13]. He did not say that Paul's writings would lead us into all truth, did He? He said that He would, through God's Holy Spirit in us.

The main purpose of the Bible is to aid in revealing God's nature to mankind and to show how He deals with mankind. The main purpose is not to be an infallible rule of conduct. That is just a sideline. The Bible is only one of the ways He has chosen to reveal Himself to mankind.[1]

Some Christians are going around the world making false claims about the Bible. This is mainly the fault of fundamentalists. We can expect it from them because they have never allowed God to seal the covenant with them. [They have not received the Baptism of the Holy Ghost.] But, the Pentecostals are the most amazing, since we have allowed God to confirm the covenant by accepting His Holy Spirit to live in us. Yet many of us are still clinging to this false infallibility teaching.

----

1. *The Heavens Declare...* (Impact Books, Inc. 137 W. Jefferson Kirkwood, MO 63122) offers an insight into one of the other ways God has chosen to reveal Himself.

How can we have let ourselves be duped into believing such a false doctrine as the inerrancy of the English version of the Bible? This book is so loaded with mistakes that it does not take much of a scholar to find some of them. Acts 12:4 is the most obvious mistake I found, where the word "Easter" is used instead of the correct word "Passover."

We have to realize and believe that it is not important that our version of the English Bible be without error. If it were without error then it would be as good as God. You say, "But the Bible is God's Word." God's Word is *contained* in the Bible, but everything in the Bible is not God's Word. Sure, He may have wanted us to see it, but much of it He did not say, or does not apply to us. So, we have to be able to pick out which parts apply, and which parts do not.

The main reason people have clung so tightly to the English version of the Bible, other than the Roman Catholic programming, is because people saw no other way to interpret the Bible without taking it literally. Which comes down to the fact that their beliefs stem from insecurity and ignorance, rather than the leading of the Holy Spirit. Seemingly, no one has been able to come up with a system of interpretation which is simple, that would allow everybody to interpret the Bible correctly no matter when or where they lived.

Too many Christians are caught up in ritual and traditional teachings that are hindering their growth. To say that the Mosaic Covenant applies to you is totally wrong! The interesting thing about people who preach that, is they are not following it totally anyway. They choose certain parts to go by but have arbitrarily decided not to go by other parts of it. It states very plainly that if you falter in one law, you blow the whole law. Only one man has not been guilty of that.

I want to try to clear up this controversy about how the Old Testament applies to us once and for all. According to the principles of covenanting, we know that a covenant is only in effect as long as the parties who made the covenant are still living, or the covenant is not broken. We may find an exception to this if the covenant is to be continued for other generations, but it continues only as long as the requirements are followed by those other generations. Whenever the covenant is broken, the curse comes into effect.

All we have to do is find out if the Mosaic Covenant was broken by one of the parties, and we will know if we are still obligated to it. The Israelites broke the covenant, therefore, absolving God of any obligation to the covenant. It is obvious that the curse of that covenant came into effect, leaving that part of the covenant the only part still in effect. As proof that the curse of the Mosaic covenant has come into effect, all we have to do is look at the curse spoken in Deuteronomy 27 and 28. Deuteronomy 28:36 says, "The Lord will bring you and the king whom you set over you to a nation which neither you nor your fathers have known and there you shall serve other gods - wood and stone. And you will become an astonishment, a proverb, and a byword among all the nations where the Lord will drive you."

Any student of history can see that this part of the covenant has come true when ten tribes of Israel were taken up into Assyria and the remaining two tribes were made subjects of another kingdom. This is proof that God is only obligated to see that the curse of this covenant is administered. We must keep in mind however, that God's administration of the Mosaic covenant curses had absolutely nothing to do with his "eternal covenant" or any other covenant. Understanding the characteristics of covenants is a pre-requisite for understanding the Bible.

When we as Christians read about a fig tree, we should go look it up, so that we can get a better idea of what are the characteristics of a fig tree. After all, all trees are similar, but very different. Each has its own characteristics, which are different from other trees. The same principle applies to covenants. People have read the word, *covenant*, but never stopped to investigate the characteristics surrounding the word, *covenant*. If they had, God would not have had so many problems trying to get us to believe the truth. All God wants us to do is believe the truth about Him.

You may be asking why God did not just explain covenants to us in the Bible so that we would have understood? First, He did not have the books of the Bible written to us. They were written to the people to whom they were written, then compiled later, so that others would get an opportunity to read them. The original listeners were familiar with covenants so no explanation of them was needed. It was not until centuries later that the world lost sight of the understanding of covenants.

The reason this is so important is so that we can see how the concept of sin has actually arisen out of man's concept of God, instead of being based on the facts of the attributes of God and covenants, on which the Bible is based.

As I was growing up under Pentecostal teachings, I saw how it seemed that God kept changing the rules of sin. What was considered sin one year, was not considered sin a few years later. What made God change His mind? This is a dilemma with which Christians still struggle. Where the problem exists it has everyone confused, Christian and non-Christian alike. More people would accept Jesus if we could just clear up this concept of sin and how it affects or does not affect us.

We will find that under a system, set up according to covenant principles, the rules do not change unless Jesus wants them to change. That will only be evident on an individual basis, of which no man will be able to stand in judgment. It is a system of liberty with responsibilities. It is amazing how we could have read Romans 14 for so many years and not have grasped this concept.

Paul says in Romans 14, "Receive one who is weak in the faith, but not to dispute over doubtful things. For one believes he may eat all things, but he who is weak eats only vegetables. Let not him who eats despise him who does not eat, and let not him who does not eat judge him who eats; for God has received him. Who are you to judge another's servant? To his own master he stands or falls. He will be made to stand, for God is able to make him stand.

> "One person esteems one day above another; another esteems every day alike. Let each be fully convinced in his own mind. He who observes the day, observes it to the Lord; and he who does not observe the day, to the Lord he does not observe it. He who eats, eats to the Lord, for he gives God thanks; and he who does not eat, to the Lord he does not eat, and gives God thanks. For none of us lives to himself, and no one dies to himself. For if we live, we live to the Lord; and if we die, we die to the Lord. Therefore, whether we live or die, we are the Lord's. For to this end Christ died and rose and lived again, that he might be Lord of both the dead and the living."

> "But why do you judge your brother? Or why do you show contempt for your brother? For we shall all stand before the judgment seat of Christ. For it is written: "As I live, says the Lord, every knee shall give account of himself to God. Therefore let us not judge one another anymore, but rather re-

solve this, not to put a stumbling block of a cause to fall in another brother's way.

"I know and am convinced by the Lord Jesus that there is nothing unclean of itself; but to him who considers anything to be unclean, to him it is unclean. Yet if your brother is grieved because of your food, you are no longer walking in love. Do not destroy with your food the one for whom Christ died.

"Therefore do not let your good be spoken of as evil; for the Kingdom of God is not food and drink, but righteousness and peace and joy in the Holy Spirit. For he who serves Christ in these things is acceptable to God and approved by men. Therefore let us pursue the things which make for peace and the things by which one may edify another.

"Do not destroy the work of God for the sake of food. All things indeed are pure, but it is evil for the man who eats with offense. It is good neither to eat meat nor drink wine nor do anything by which your brother stumbles or is offended or is made weak. Do you have faith? Have it to yourself before God. Happy is he who does not condemn himself in what he approves. But he who doubts is condemned if he eats, because he does not eat from faith; for whatever is not from faith is sin.

"We then who are strong ought to bear with the scruples of the weak, and not to please ourselves. Let each of us please his neighbor for his good, leading to edification. For even Christ did not please himself; but as it is written, 'the reproaches of those who reproach you fell on me.' For whatever things were written before were written for our learning, that we through the patience and comfort of the scriptures might have hope. Now may the God of patience and comfort grant you to be like minded toward one another, according to Christ Jesus, that you may with one mind and one mouth glorify the God and Father of our Lord Jesus Christ." (Romans 14:1-15:6)

"All things are lawful for me, but all things are not helpful. All things are lawful for me, but I will not be brought under the power of any." (I Corinthians 6:12) "Now concerning things offered to idols: We know that we all have knowledge. Knowledge puffs up, but love edifies. And if anyone thinks that he knows anything, he knows nothing yet as he ought to know. But if anyone knows God, this one is known by Him. Therefore concerning the eating of things offered to idols, we know that an idol is nothing in the world, and that there is no other God but one. For even if there are so called gods, whether in heaven or on earth (as there are many gods and many lords), yet for us there is only one God, the Father, of whom are all things, and we for Him; and one Lord Jesus Christ, through whom are all things, and through whom we live.

"However, there is not in everyone that knowledge; for some, with consciousness of the idol, until now even as a thing offered to an idol; and their conscience being weak, is defiled. But food does not commend us to God; for neither if we eat are we the better, nor if we do not eat are we the worse. But beware lest somehow this liberty of yours become a stumbling block to those who are weak.

"For if anyone sees you who have knowledge eating in an idol's temple, will not the conscience of him who is weak be embolden to eat those things offered to idols? And because of your knowledge shall the weaker brother perish, for whom Christ died? But when you thus sin against the brethren, and wound their weak conscience, you sin against Christ. Therefore, if food makes my brother stumble, I will never again eat meat, lest I make my brother stumble." (I Corinthians 8:1-13)

The point I wanted to make concerns liberty, but we had to look at the whole chapter to understand what it was talking about. Notice also that it spoke about causing your brother to stumble by openly displaying your liberty. That is why I say *liberty with responsibility*. Let us look at some more verses dealing with liberty.

"All things are lawful for me, but all things are not helpful; all things are lawful for me, but all things do not edify. Let no one seek his own, but each one the other's well-being. Eat whatever is sold in the meat market, asking no questions for conscience sake; for 'the Earth is the Lord's and all its fullness.' If any of those who do not believe invite you to dinner, and you desire to go, eat whatever is set before you asking no question for conscience sake. But if anyone says to you, 'This was offered to idols,' do not eat it for the sake of the one who told you and for conscience sake, for 'the Earth is the Lord's and all its fullness.' Conscience, I say not your own, but that of the other. For why is my liberty judged by another man's conscience? But if I partake with thanks, why am I evil spoken of for the food over which I give thanks? Therefore, whether you eat or drink or whatever you do, do all to the glory of God. Give no offense either to the Jews or the Greeks or to the Church of God;" (I Corinthians 10:23-32)

"Now the Lord is the Spirit; and where the Spirit of the Lord is there is liberty." (II Corinthians 2:17)

"Stand fast therefore in the liberty by which Christ has made us free, and do not be entangled again with a yoke of bondage...For you, brethren have been called to liberty; only do not use liberty as an opportunity for the flesh, but through love serve one another." (Galatians 5:1 & 13)

"Therefore, let no one judge you in food or in drink, or regarding a festival or a new moon, or sabbaths, which are a shadow of things to come, but the substance is of Christ. Let no one defraud you of your reward, taking delight into those things which he has not seen, vainly puffed up by his fleshly mind, not holding fast to the Head, from whom all the body, nourished and knit together by joints and ligaments, grows with the increase which is from God." (Colossians 2:16-17)

"Therefore, if you died with Christ from the basic principles of the world, why as though living in the world, do you subject yourselves to regulations--'do not touch, do not taste, do not handle,'--which all concern things which perish with the using according to the commandments of men? These things indeed have an appearance of wisdom in self-imposed religion, false humility, and neglect of the body, but are of no value against the indulgence of the flesh." (Colossians 2:20-23)

After reading all these verses, it is difficult to understand how Christians could have debated this subject for so many years. Let us set the record straight at this time so the conflicts will cease. This idea of liberty in Jesus is based on a covenant principle that has existed a lot longer than our Bible. The principle says that when two parties come into a covenant relationship with each other, the other party is allowed to make demands, or rules, binding on the other party. Since this covenant is entered into of their own free will, because of their love for each other, neither party would demand anything which might offend the covenant partner. Only the parties involved in the covenant are allowed to make demands in this covenant relationship.

Now, let's put this background information into perspective in regard to our relationship with Jesus. In order to be born-again, "you gave your life to Jesus," or as some say, "you gave your heart to Jesus." Since history tells us that these terms are covenant terms that have been used for centuries, we know that we made a covenant with Jesus. This means then, that in your relationship with God, only Jesus is allowed to make demands of you. No one, not even the Bible writers, are allowed to tell you what to do in your spiritual relationship with Him. This is proven historically by studying the history of covenants. The way that Jesus makes demands is by God's Holy Spirit that goes along with the covenant gift-giving, if accepted by Jesus' covenant partner.

But, we still need to sift through this subject of sin and its connection with God's forgiveness and the born-again experience. As we saw earlier, mankind, since Adam and Eve, were born with corrupted blood, which, really was a sin nature. Since we were all born with this sin-nature, we can then understand why people are bound by sin. With some people that sin-nature is more evident than with other people.

To really understand this idea of sin, we need to recognize what causes it. As indicated above, sin can be a result of a sin-nature within a person, where the physical part of a person is controlled by their spirit within them. In the life of a Christian, this same principle holds true after a person becomes born-again and should be the desire, or mark, to shoot at. However, at times the opposite is true where the physical part of a person overrides the spirit within.

Most times we have no excuse for sin. We are drawn into it by our own desires. These desires may be for things even the world considers sinful such as adultery, revenge, murder, taking what is not ours, or they may be small, such as an extra helping of food, one drink too many, an extra few minutes of sleep, one more business deal to close, etc.

The only other way that sin will be able to come to

the fore is by demonic activity, whether by possession or oppression. Either way, demonic activity is the most difficult to control and is a significant cause of what we see as sin today. It can only be controlled by the authority of Jesus, to which born-again people have access. Demonic oppression, on the other hand, is an unseen force much like a blanket which comes upon a person, that usually lights upon the shoulder area of a person and the person immediately has the feeling of heaviness and the characteristic of the demon spirit. The two oppressions I have "felt" at different times have been a spirit of homosexuality and a spirit of fear. Some other oppressive spirits are: lust, bulemia, anorexia, and different phobias.

The most important thing for a person to do when accosted by a heaviness and a totally different and unnatural feeling coming upon them is to resist it immediately. Rebuke it, in the name of Jesus, then make a hasty exit from that area. Do not consider accepting that feeling as natural. Resist it, and it will flee from you.

Another important point that we need to realize about sin, is that sin, like a habit, binds a person. There is no true freedom until we gain release from the sins that bind us. Contrary to popular opinion, sinning does not send us to eternal damnation. Sinning keeps us from enjoying true freedom in this life. What we need to realize is that every cell in our body cries out for freedom, thus causing a war within ourselves.

Hopefully this chapter has cleared up a lot of questions about this subject of sin. Sin is bad! It is bad because it keeps us bound up from receiving all that God has for us. Just because sin will not send us to Hell, does not absolve us from the consequences that go along with continuing in sin. The consequences are that any sin adversely affects us and those around us. Just think of any so-called sin: drinking, smoking, adultery, partying, etc., then picture how doing these things will affect you and those around you. The effects cause a separation, whether that be physical, emotional, or mental. Always a separation is evident, it just takes on a different form with each different sin. The Bible was correct when it said, "the wages of sin is separation [death]." It is separation, but not eternal damnation.

6

ATONEMENT, WHAT'S THAT?

Atonement is usually considered an Old Testament, Hebrew term that does not get much play in the New Testament in its regular spelling, "atonement." In the New Testament the word "reconcile" is used instead. The two terms are basically synonymous and are often interchanged.

Usually the word is defined as the covering for sin. This definition is taken from the Old Testament, or Old Covenant ceremony whereby the sins of the people were atoned for, or covered by the blood of the sacrifice. This definition for Old Covenant sacrifices is fairly accurate because they were just a "shadow of things to come."

That is not exactly an accurate, or adequate, defini-tion of "the things to come," which was what Jesus did on the cross. Jesus' blood shed at the cross did not cover the sins of mankind, but actually, blasted it out of the way. Which brings us to a more correct definition of the word, "atonement," in relationship to what Jesus did.

The New Covenant use of the word expresses a restored, harmonious relationship, or refers to the act that brought about the restored relationship. The Greek word, *katallage*, also translated reconcile, shows that a certain harmonious relationship existed at some point in time, and a restoring, or reconciliation was necessary. We already know that Adam and Eve transgressed, immediately prompting God, the Creator, to initiate an atonement, or reconciliation.

When researching the subject of who or what caused an estrangement between God and mankind, we find very little evidence to prove that it was caused by Adam and Eve. Yet we find this teaching historically accepted by Christianity as fact. What is not as readily accepted as fact is the overwhelming amount of evidence proving that the reconciliation is also an historical fact. So far as this subject of atonement is concerned, historically, the Armenian theology teaches that the atonement effected by Jesus, pertains only to those who believe it. Calvinists, on the other hand, believe the atonement was only for the elect of God. Almost never in Christian writings do we see the idea of the universalism of atonement for all of mankind. The German scholar Johannes Cocceius, in the 17th century, for one, taught it from a covenant standpoint that Jesus' covenant made atonement for all of mankind.

A very popular definition of the word atonement is "at-one-ment." It brings about a position of at-one-ment. At-one-ment is probably the easiest way to remember the definition, and it is for the most part an accurate expression of what Jesus did. Some of the Greek words closely associated with this word are forms of *hilaskomai*--to make propitiation; or to make reconciliation; to atone for; and the verb *katallasso,* meaning to reconcile. In Trumbull's, *The Blood Covenant*, we find a slightly different definition that sheds some light on the subject. "Yet again Hamburger, one of the foremost rabbinical authorities of the present day [19th century] insists that the very word for "atonement," in the Hebrew, commonly taken to mean "a cover," or "a covering;" has in it more properly the idea of a compassioned union, or an "at-one-ment." He says: 'I hold the word *kaphar*, in the sense "to pitch" (to overlay with pitch, Genesis 6:14) "to fill up the seam" ("to close up the chasm"), as a symbolic expression for the reunion of the sinner with God. And it is not the flesh of the sacrifice, but the blood, that God counts the atonement, or the means of at-one-ment between the sinner and Himself.' (*The Blood Covenant*, p. 352, [Trumbull's reference to the author Hamburger was taken from the *Real Encyclopedie* f. *Bibel u. Talmud, I.*, p. 80]) "All the detailed requirements of the Mosaic ritual, and all the specific teachings of the Rabbis, as well, go to show the pre-eminence of the blood in the sacrificial offerings; go to show, that it is the life (which the blood is), and not the death (which is merely necessary to the securing of the blood), of the victim, that is the means of atonement..." (*The Blood Covenant*, p. 245)

"Atonement, salvation, rescue, redemption is by the blood, the life of Christ; not by his death as such; not by His broken body in itself; but by that blood which was given at the inevitable cost of his broken body and of His death." (*The Blood Covenant*, p. 287)

The only New Testament verse in which the King James Version uses the term atonement is Romans 5:11, "And not only so, but we also joy in God through our Lord Jesus Christ, by whom we have now received the atonement." Most other versions at which I have looked use the word reconciliation.

William Beck, in his translation of the New Testament, used the word "friendship." Any one of the three words is an adequate translation as we will see. In the New Englishman's Greek Concordance and Lexicon, the Greek word is defined as "a reconciliation," or "restoration to favor." (*The New Testament In The Language Of Today*, William F. Beck, Concordia Publishing House), (*The New Englishman's Greek Concordance And Lexicon*, George V. Wigram & Jay P. Green, Sr.)

Another lexicon defines the same Greek word as (1) exchange; of the business of moneychangers, exchanging equivalent values. (2) adjustment of a difference, reconciliation, restoration to favor. (*The New Englishman's Greek Concordance And Lexicon*, p. 333)

Christians have had an erroneous teaching about the word "saved" because of a lack of understanding of the word "reconciled." If we had just taken a dictionary and defined the word, then believed the definition, we would have not been so wrong in our theology.

Romans 5:10 says, "For if when we were enemies we were reconciled to God through the death of His Son, much more, having been reconciled, we shall be saved by His life." We can see by this verse that we, as human beings, were reconciled to God by the death of Jesus. If we (human being) were brought back into a position of friendly relations with God by the death of Jesus, then that tells us, from His standpoint, He is on friendly relations with all of mankind. According to this verse, God does not make His peace with us when we get "saved," but rather He made peace with us by Jesus' death. So the statement that God makes peace with us when we get "saved" is erroneous.

To analyze this verse, Romans 5:10, more closely, we need to know why we (mankind, as a whole) and God were enemies. We need to remember what Adam and Eve did to get us into this position of estrangement. They transgressed a law of their covenant with God; and the rest of mankind, with a few exceptions, treated God as our enemy. We acted as if God was our enemy, as if God had something against us, when all the time, He was just an innocent bystander.

So, if God was the innocent one (the one who was offended by Adam and Eve), then if He felt like coming back into friendly relations with us, He could of His own free will, declare we were on friendly terms again. He did not have to wait for our consent to declare the enmity between us, from His side of it, as no longer existing. He could just declare the fact that He had no enmity against us at all, if He wanted to do it. Whether or not we reciprocated by declaring the enmity from our side of it as null and void would not necessarily have any effect on His decision. It could have had an effect on His decision to hold against us the bad feelings that we had toward Him, but He decided He would not hold that against us. He can do whatever He wants to do. If He decided to be reconciled to us, not basing His decision on our wanting to be reconciled to Him, He is able to do that since He was the one offended.

This is one of the main reasons for incorrect teaching in this area. Most Christians have never looked at the subject of which party did the offending and which party was offended. It is obvious that Adam and Eve did the offending and God was the offended party. Adam and Eve caused the enmity, or estrangement. The rest of mankind was just involuntarily, or voluntarily, led into this enmity with God, not by what we did, but by what was on the inside of us, a dead (separated) spirit. The enmity we felt toward God was caused by what was on the inside of us that we had no control over. If we had no control over it, because we were born with it, then for God to hold it against us would be very unfair.

We should be able to see now why we were enemies and why a reconciliation was necessary. On God's part, we have been reconciled to Him just because He decided to do it. Now, He wants to be reconciled to us, and that depends upon our deciding to stop fighting Him, so that we can become friends with God. That happens when we get "saved." At that time, He becomes reconciled to us, *not us to Him,* as it has been taught. Look at what Romans 5:11 says, "And not only that, but we also rejoice in God through our Lord Jesus Christ, through whom we have now received the reconciliation."

77

It speaks of the reconciliation in past tense, just what I said earlier. The reconciliation, to quote E. C. Blackman, "is not a process, but a completed act."[1] It can not be said any more clearly than that. The reconciliation is past tense.

II Corinthians 5:18-19 goes right along with Romans 5:10-11, "Now all things are of God, who has reconciled us to Himself through Jesus Christ, and has given us the ministry of reconciliation, that is that God was in Christ reconciling the world to Himself, not imputing their trespasses to them, and has committed to us the word of reconciliation."

The first verse says that He reconciled "us" to Himself, but that does not infer that "us" is inclusive of just Christians. The second verse is all inclusive as it says "reconciling the world to Himself."

In the second verse, God even had Paul say that God was "not imputing their trespasses against them." Imputing means attributing or ascribing, making the verse to read that God was "not attributing their trespasses to them." He was attributing their trespasses to Jesus. He was not holding it against them. Then Paul ends both of these verses by saying that God wanted us to tell the world about the reconciliation which took place at the cross.

"For it pleased the Father that in Him (Jesus) all the fullness should dwell, and by Him (Jesus) to reconcile all things to Himself, by Him (Jesus), whether things on Earth or things in Heaven, having made peace through the blood of His (Jesus') cross. And you, who once were

----

1. The author apologizes that he does not remember the exact source from which this quote was taken.

78

alienated and enemies in your mind by wicked works, yet now He has reconciled [fully] in the body of His flesh through death, to present you holy, and blameless, and irreproachable in His sight..." (Colossians 1:19-22) These verses also only indicate a reconciliation for all of mankind, not just those that accept it.

It appears that verse 23 means that you are only reconciled, "if you indeed continue in the faith, grounded and steadfast, and are not moved away from the hope of the gospel which you heard, which was preached to every creature under Heaven, of which I, Paul, became a minister." This verse has nothing to do with the reconciliation. It has to do with the latter part of verse 22, "to present you holy, and blameless, and irreproachable in His sight..." It has to do with a believer moving away from the truth (gospel), not a person who has never heard the gospel.

A verse that corresponds with Colossians 1:20 is Ephesians 1:10, "that in the dispensation of the fullness of times He might gather together in one all things in Christ, both which are in heaven and which are on earth - in Him." This is referring to the reconciliation that took place at one point in time. It is not happening at each altar call, or when a person is "saved."

In regard to the reconciling of the world, let us read what Romans 11:15 says. "For if their [Israel] being cast away is the reconciling of the world, what would their acceptance be but life from the dead?" The world has been reconciled to God, because Israel has been cast away, in respect to their covenant with Him.

At this time I would like to briefly mention the term "propitiation." This is one word in the New Testament that has been mistranslated probably as much as any other word. It should have been translated "expiation," which is what the Hebrews believed the word was.

The Greeks used the word "propitiation" because propitiation basically means "to appease," and the Greeks were accustomed to doing that. The Hebrew people, on the other hand, were believers in expiation which is a complete appeaser, or totally wiping out any conflict as if it never happened. Not so with appeasement. Had we read the reference for propitiation in the *Interpreter's Dictionary*, "propitiation" means to appease, in a more general sense, or to entreat the favor of someone. *The Interpreter's Dictionary of the Bible* was totally correct when they said that the Septuagent translators generally used the Greek word to express the divine removal of guilt or defilement and clearly regard their pagan meaning of "propitiating deity" as inappropriate to the religion of Israel, because there is nowhere in the New Testament that the idea of propitiation occurs. It is the Greek pagan religion that teaches that God can be appeased.

However, God cannot be appeased. His wrath against mankind can be expiated, or totally wiped out, or completely appeased, which is a good definition of expiation, but never, never, ever propitiated. If we take that definition of propitiation and make it expiation, which means to be completely appeased, we can now look at how the word propitiation is used in the New Testament. We find it in Romans 3:25;

> "...being justified freely by His grace through the redemption that is in Christ Jesus, whom God set forth to be a propitiation (expiation) by His blood, through faith, to demonstrate His righteousness because in His forbearance God had passed over the sins that were previously committed." (Romans 3:24-25)

> "And He, Himself is the propitiation (expiation) for our sins and not for ours only but also for the whole world." (I John 2:2); "And this is love (agape), not that we loved (agape) God, but that He loved

(agape) us and sent His son to be the propitiation (expiation) for our sins." (I John 4:10)

We can see in these two verses, that Jesus was the complete appeaser for our sins. Not only for the sins of Christians, but also for the whole world. Verse 2 of Chapter 2 says this specifically, and not for ours only but also for the whole world, meaning not for Christians only, but also for the whole world. That Jesus was the complete appeaser for all the world's sins. Why is it that Christians could not have read that verse and believed it? It totally lines up with what the rest of the Bible has to say.

I will conclude this discussion of reconciliation by referring to Ephesians 2:11-16.

"Therefore remember that you, once Gentiles in the flesh--who are called uncircumcision by what is called the circumcision made in the flesh with hands--that at that time you were without Christ being aliens from the commonwealth of Israel and strangers from the covenants of promise, having no hope and without God in the world. But now in Christ Jesus you who were once far off have been made near by the blood of Christ."

"For He Himself is our peace, who has made both [circumcised and uncircumcised] one, and has broken down the middle wall of division between us having abolished in His flesh the enmity, that is, the law of commandments contained in ordinances, so as to create in Himself one new man from the two, thus making peace, and that He might reconcile them both to God in one body through the cross, thereby putting to death the enmity."

In none of these verses using the same Greek word, or the word reconcile, does it say or imply that a person will receive the atonement, or reconciliation if they accept it. What these verses really say is that the atonement, the closing up of the chasm between God and man, the reconciliation, was accomplished by what Jesus did, therefore leaving absolutely nothing by which we can affect the result of that atonement.

7

JUSTIFICATION? BY WHOSE FAITH?

The word that Protestants have really misunderstood is the word "justification." Or, maybe I should clarify that by saying that we were only confused as to the "means of justification." Had we just read what the Bible said about it, and not what Martin Luther said about it, there would have been no confusion. Mr. Luther was confused about it, which started the interpretation that has characterized the Protestant church's view of justification. Martin Luther was confused because be came out of the Roman Catholic system, which teaches a "justification by your own works" program. Because he was so far ahead of the rest of the theologians, God was probably overjoyed to find someone to "break away from the pack," so to speak. In my opinion, God wanted to use Luther as a springboard for others to move on to greater revelation. But, too many people blindly follow Luther and other men without discovering what is wrong with their teachings.

We first must establish the meaning of "justification" before we can get a handle on what the Bible says about it. It is a forensic, or legal term that simply means to be declared not guilty. It does not mean to be "found" not guilty, only to be declared not guilty. The former means that you never committed a crime, or at least no evidence was found for a conviction. The latter, however, means that you could have been guilty, but were judged as not guilty. For a judge to declare someone not guilty in a legal situation yet maintain his reputation as a

just and competent judge, there had to arise some miti-
gating circumstances.

Now, we have seen earlier that mankind was guilty
because of what Adam and Eve did. Mankind was
considered guilty until they, or someone else, took the
punishment, whereby mankind could then legally be
declared "not guilty." According to Romans 8:33 and
Romans 4:5, God is the one doing the justifying, or the
declaring of who is and who is not guilty. No one else
gets this privilege, or has this responsibility. God alone
has the responsibility to either justly or unjustly declare
guilt or innocence.

We need to discover the reason why, or if, He
declares not guilty [justify], and also we must establish
who is declared not guilty. These are the questions most
of us have never answered, therefore leaving us preaching the wrong gospel.

By studying the Old Testament, and the gospels, we
see that the Israelites were attempting to be justified by
their observance of the Mosaic law. It was never God's
intention to declare them not guilty just because they
followed the law, as it was virtually impossible to follow
every aspect of that law. He wanted them to recognize
the futility of it all. Finally, He was able to get Paul the
Apostle to know that justification was up to God, and it
only came by faith, not by works.

"Therefore, we conclude that a man is justified by
faith apart from the deeds of the law...since there is one
god who would justify the circumcised by faith and the
uncircumcised through faith." (Romans 3:28-30) These
verses tell us that being declared not guilty comes by
faith. Whose faith it is has not as yet been established.
To go along with these verses we have Galatians 3:10 &
12. "For as many as are of the works of the law are
under the curse; for it is written, 'Cursed is everyone

who does not continue in all things which are written in the book of the law, to do them.' But that no one is justified by law in the sight of God is evident, for the just shall live by faith. Yet the law is not of faith, but the man who does them shall live by [in] them. Therefore, the law was our tutor to bring us to Christ, that we might be justified by faith." (Galatians 3:24)

Why have Christians not believed Romans 3:25, "Who [Jesus] was delivered up because of our offenses, and was raised because of [for] our justification." It puts the situation very simply. Jesus was put on the cross to suffer because of our [mankind's] offenses. He was raised because we were declared not guilty. This verse is one of the best verses for clarifying what happened at the cross and the tomb.

The New King James Version uses the word "because" as a conjunction for both the offenses and the justification. The word "because" indicates that the action was past tense, a causative action. One event caused, or resulted in, another event. This verse indicates that our offenses caused the delivering up of Jesus, and our "not guiltiness" caused Jesus to be resurrected. I am not saying that it was not God's power that caused the resurrection, because it was. The state of "not guiltiness" allowed all things to line up so that God's Spirit could raise Jesus from the dead.

There is one other way of looking at this verse 25, by interpreting the word "our" as referring to Christians only. "Now it was not written for His sake alone that it was imputed to him, but also for us. It shall be imputed to us who believe in Him who raised up Jesus our Lord from the dead, who was delivered up because of our offenses, and raised because of our justification." (Romans 4:23-25) A person could almost read these verses as pertaining to Christians only because verse 24 says, "It shall be imputed to us who believe in Him..."

This is a true statement but not a statement of truth, or an all inclusive statement. Just because the verse only mentions believers does not exclude unbelievers from justification.

To interpret these verses as "believers only" verses is also to say that Jesus was delivered up because of the offenses of believers only and not for the offenses of the rest of the world. That is the only way to keep verse 25 consistent. If the resurrection was the result of the justification of believers only, then the delivering up, also, was because of the offenses of only believers. Ridiculous! Verse 25 can only be correctly interpreted one way, that is that Jesus was delivered up because of the offenses of the whole world and then Jesus was resurrected because the whole world has been declared not guilty [justified]!

We will see this more clearly when we look at the word redemption, in that, what Jesus did on the cross cannot be divided between the have, and the have-nots. It is difficult for me to prove that point with the word, justification, but it is undeniable, when put with redemption, atonement, propitiation, etc.

Romans Chapter 5 has several verses concerning justification.

"Therefore having been justified by faith, we have peace with God through our Lord Jesus Christ, through whom we have access by faith into this grace in which we stand and rejoice and hope in the glory of God."

"Much more then, having now been justified [declared not guilty] by His blood, we shall be saved from wrath through Him."(5:9) "And the gift is not like that which came through the one who sinned. For the judgment which came from one offense resulted in condemnation, but the free gift which came from many offenses resulted in justification." "For if by the one man's offense death reigned through the one, much more those who receive abundance of grace and of the gift of righteousness will reign in life through the One, Jesus Christ. (Therefore, as through one man's offense judgment came to all men, resulting in condemnation, even so through one man's righteous act the free gift came to all men, resulting in justification of life.)" Romans (5:16-18)

Reviewing these verses in Romans 5, we find that mankind is declared not guilty [justified] by faith (vs.1), by Jesus' blood (vs.9), and the free gift (vs.16&18). Anyone studying church history knows that Romans 5:1 is a hydrogen bomb in the theological arsenal of evangelicals, because they have been misled to believe that the faith spoken of is their own faith. However, the verse never says, or even implies that. It only says faith, and never clarifies whose faith is responsible for the justification.

Verse 9 makes it clear that justification could not come from a person's own faith because it says that justification came by way of Jesus' blood. It does not say that justification came by way of our acceptance of that blood. So, if the declaration of not guilty came, as verse 9 says, "by Jesus' blood," then in order for verse 1 to remain consistent with verse 9, it must refer to someone's faith other than our own.

How then, does the free gift in verses 16 and 18 figure into this discussion? Let us look at it this way. A free gift is free whether you do anything about it or not. You can do nothing to earn it. It is given with no strings attached. Even if the free gift is not accepted, it remains a free gift, unless taken back by the giver. It appears that verses 16 and 18 are saying that mankind's "not guiltiness" is the result of a free gift given without obligation to an undeserving mankind.

We can conclude then that if the "not guiltiness" is a free gift, and God is the one responsible for declaring a person guilty or not guilty, as established earlier, then it follows that He is the one giving the free gift. If it is His gift to give, then it is His prerogative to declare "not guiltiness" for whomever He desires. He desired to do so for us, so He did. He declared us not guilty when He declared Jesus guilty in our place.

We need to see if the other verses dealing with justification are consistent with these verses at which we have just looked. Romans 3:24 says, "Being justified freely by His grace through the redemption that is in Christ Jesus." If we study the word grace we will find that it means unmerited favor, or unmerited divine favor. Remembering what we said earlier about the free gift being undeserved, we can conclude that grace and the free gift are synonymous; therefore, making grace available to all and applying to all of mankind, *not just those who believe.*

We Christians believed that justification applied only to us. The Bible does not say nor imply that. To think that we could change an historical event such as God's declaration that all of mankind is not guilty is ridiculous and boastful. How could He have possibly divided the act of justification into the haves and the have-nots?

I want to review the subject of justification. First of all, biblical justification means "to be declared not guilty," even though we were guilty. Secondly, God the Creator of the universe, is the one who decides who is, and who is not, declared not guilty. Third, we cannot earn the status of not guilty by obeying the Mosaic law or any other law. Fourth, we found that, according to

Romans 4:25, Jesus was raised because of our having been declared not guilty. Fifth, according to Romans 5:9, we were declared not guilty by Jesus' blood, not our acceptance of the blood. Sixth, we were declared not guilty by faith, however, it does not say by whose faith the justification came. Seventh, our "not guiltiness" was the result of a free gift. Eighth, Romans 3:24 says that we are justified freely by God's grace, or unmerited favor.

In all of these verses, we find nothing to support Protestantism's claim that a person is justified by their own faith. It should be quite obvious by now that the "declaration of not guilty" came as the result of an event totally independent of anything that a person does or does not do. We should have concluded by now that we cannot affect our status with God, as He has already declared us not guilty!!

8

REDEEMED FROM

SATAN'S POWER OR GOD'S WRATH?

Redemption is the legal process by which a person, or thing, is bought back for its original owner, or to its original state. For instance, a person falling into slavery due to inability to pay a debt, could rely on his next of kin to "redeem" him (buy back) from slavery. The next of kin, if means were available, was obligated to pay the debt. The idea of redeemer and next of kin is so closely related, that the Hebrew word *goel* can be translated either way. (Study also the concept of avenger of blood to get more insight into the word *goel*.) This word is used in several places in the Old Testament to describe the relationship of the Hebrews and God. In one of the many Bible dictionaries, it states that there is the implication in the idea that the *goel* rescues that which was forfeited and restores justice to those who are not in a position to help themselves.

One of the most interesting, and tearful, stories I came across while researching the subject of redemption was the story of a father from a Middle Eastern country. His son was intentionally killed by someone from another family, therefore making it necessary to avenge the blood of his son. Being the next of kin, or nearest kin, the father, customarily, could have chosen payment in blood or money. If he chose blood, he could demand the blood of an animal or human blood. In the case of the father, he demanded that a sheep be brought to him by the offending family. When delivered, this father slit the throat of the sheep and let the animal's blood cover the ground at his feet. While doing so, the father, with words, assured the offending family that the blood of the sheep canceled-out the blood of his son. I know it sounds crazy! This type of thinking is contrary to our Western civilization programming we have been subjected to all our lives.

I am going to again quote from H. Clay Trumbull's *The Blood Covenant*, page 259-260. I am doing this because he did his research of Middle Eastern customs in the 19th century at a time when those customs had not changed very much in thousands of years. My research of other sources lined up with the basic writings of Trumbull, and with his book readily accessible, readers will be able to double check what I am saying.

"Another gleam of the primitive truth, that blood is life and not death, and that the transference of blood is the transference of life, is found in the various Mosaic references to the *goel,* the person who is authorized to obtain blood for blood as an act of justice, in the East. And another proof of the prevailing error in the Western mind, through confounding blood with death, and justice with punishment, is the common rendering of the term *goel*, as avenger; or revenger; in our English Bible, wherever that term applies to the balancing of blood account; although the same Hebrew word is in other connections commonly translated "redeemer," or "ransomer."

"The term *goel,* was applied to that kinsman whose duty it was to secure justice to the injured, and to restore, as it were, a normal balance to the disturbed family relations." (p. 260) "In the event of a depletion of the family by the loss of blood--the loss of a life--the *goel* had a responsibility of securing to the family an equivalent of that loss, by other blood, or by an agreed payment for its value. His mission was not vengeance, but equity. He was not an avenger, but a redeemer, a restorer, a balancer. In this light, and in this light alone, are all the Oriental customs in connection with blood canceling seen to be consistent." (p. 260)

"And even where the blood of the slayer is insisted on, there are often found indications that the purpose of this choice rests on the primitive belief that the lost life is made good to the depleted family by the newly received blood." (p. 262-263) "...it is evident that the primal idea of the *goel's* mission was to restore life for life, or to secure the adjusted equivalent of a lost life; not to wreak vengeance, nor yet to mete out punishment." (p. 263)

We have got to follow this now. How this was so ingrained in these people of that day! We have to look at it in its historical setting, and we who are from Western cultures need to forget our Western ideas of prison terms and other punishments. We have to look at it in the Middle Eastern, or the Oriental, mind as to what was their definition of redeem and redemption. If we study history, we will find many different references to the idea of redemption, to the idea of redeeming and being redeemed, a person's life being redeemed by the blood of an animal being shed in place of that blood of the victim. Now, this practice may sound strange, but that is the way it was.

The basic custom we need to understand is this, when a person was offended, when a member of your family was killed, then you had a right to accept payment in money, which could be considered blood money, or you had a right to demand blood in payment for the blood that was shed in your family. Whichever one of those you chose, whether blood or money, you could only choose one, and once you chose you had no right to demand any more payment. No right at all! So, we need to follow this custom and take that as our definition of redemption and apply that to what the Bible says.

Many of us have confused this idea of redemption because we have had to function under the false teaching that Jesus paid that redemptive price to Satan. There has been a story going around on radio shows, and elsewhere, about Jesus and Satan making a deal to buy back mankind from Satan. Jesus was buying back mankind from eternal punishment from God, not Satan. You see, God, the creator of the universe, was the one who was offended, not Satan. In the Garden of Eden, Adam and Eve were the ones who caused the offense and they did it against God. They offended Him, therefore, God was the one who had the right to demand payment, not Satan. We have had this backwards. Had we not gotten it backwards, we would not have the problem with believing that Jesus did it all for us. We have to realize that Jesus paid the price to God the Father. When he paid the price, God only had the right to demand one payment. That is what God set up in the beginning before the foundation of the earth. There was only one payment that could be made, that could be demanded by God, and He made the demand in blood, not in money.

What we have to figure out are the answers to the following questions. Was that payment made? Was that payment accepted? If it was made and accepted by God, then He has no right to demand any other payment. Therefore, He cannot demand that somebody has to spend eternity separated from Him, because the payment for that person's offenses has already been paid. Are you following that? It is fairly simple, so I hope it does not take you as long as it took me to catch this principle. All we have to do is figure out who the payment was made to. The payment is always made to the offended party. That is elementary. It is an historical fact that is inescapable.

It is obvious. Genesis, Chapter 3 tells us that God the Creator, was the offended party, not Satan. Therefore, the payment was paid to Him. The payment, according to your Bible, was paid by Jesus Christ. It was not paid by Buddha, or Confucius, or Mohammed, or Rev. Moon, or Jimmy Swaggart, or Oral Roberts, or anybody else who ever lived. The payment was made only by Jesus Christ and did God accept that payment? The answer is written throughout the whole New Testament, and several places in the Old Testament, that God accepted that payment. Isaiah Chapter 53 is strong evidence that God the Father "saw the travail of His soul, and was satisfied!" That God has no right to demand another payment from any other person is the historical fact.

Having built a foundation under the subject of redemption, as it applies to Jesus, we now should see what the New Testament says about it. We will start with:

> "...being justified freely by His grace through the redemption that is in Christ Jesus..." (Romans 3:24); "But of Him you are in Christ Jesus, who became for us wisdom from God--and righteousness and sanctification and redemption--" (I Corinthians 1:30); "Christ has redeemed us from the curse of the law, having become a curse for us (for it is written, 'Cursed is everyone who hangs on a tree')," (Galatians 3:13); "to redeem those who were under the law, that we might receive the adoption as sons." (Galatians 4:5); "In Him we have redemption through His blood, the forgiveness of sins, according to the riches of His grace," (Ephesians 1:7); "who is the guarantee of our inheritance until the redemption of the purchased possession, to the praise of His glory." (Ephesians 1:14) [Which takes us back to Acts 20:28;] "Therefore take heed to yourselves and to all the flock, among which the Holy Spirit has made you overseers, to the church

of God which He purchased with His own Blood...", "in whom we have redemption through His blood, the forgiveness of sins." (Colossians 1:14); "not with the blood of goats and calves, but with His own blood He entered the Most Holy Place once for all, having obtained eternal redemption." (Hebrews 9:12); "And for this reason He is the Mediator of the new covenant, by means of death, for the redemption of the transgressions under the first covenant, that those who are called may receive the promise of the eternal inheritance." (Hebrews 9:15)

"Knowing that you were not redeemed with corruptible things, like silver or gold, from your aimless conduct received by tradition from your fathers, but with the precious blood of Christ, as of a lamb without blemish and without spot." (I Peter 1:18-19); "And they sang a new song saying: "You are worthy to take the scroll, and to open its seals; for you were slain, and have redeemed us to God by Your blood out of every tribe and tongue and people and nation, and have made us kings and priests to our God; and we shall reign on the earth." (Revelation 5:9)

It *is* obvious. God's original blood (life) in Adam and Eve, had been lost when they transgressed the covenant they had with God. That lost blood was from God, therefore giving Him the right to demand payment in blood. It was His choice to make, and He made it, when He required that Jesus forfeit His blood to balance the account of mankind. This subject can stand alone as proof of the forgiveness of God for all of mankind.

9

GRACE - EVANGELICALS

TRY TO EARN IT

"Amazing Grace, How sweet the sound. That saved a wretch like me. I once was lost, but now am found. Was blind, but now I see! 'Twas grace that taught my heart to fear and grace my fears relieved; How precious did that grace appear the hour I first believed! Through many dangers, toils, and snares, I have already come; 'Tis grace hath brought me safe thus far, And grace will lead me home."

You have heard and/or sung this song hundreds of times. But, did you ever stop to find out what the word "grace" really means? It is another one of the Christian catch-words that has been misinterpreted by evangelicals for centuries. By just looking at how the word is used in this song, you should be able to see how the word must have different definitions because it is used to refer to different aspects of God.

Follow closely to what the word grace in this song refers. First, it refers to what it was that saved a wretch like me. Take notice that it was the grace that did the saving. If that is true, then all we have to do is get the correct definition of grace, then we will understand how we are, or were, saved. Before we discuss the definition, I want to point out some other things about this song.

The second part of verse one implies that the same grace found me and opened my eyes. In verse two, we find that it was grace that taught my heart to fear, and it was also grace that relieved my fears. Then, we see that the grace appeared precious when I believed, which could imply that the grace did not appear until I believed it, or it was always there, but I never realized it until I believed.

In verse three, we see that it is grace that has brought me through the many dangers, toils, and snares, and also, it is grace that will lead me home. Amazing, isn't it, how many different definitions this songwriter attributed to the word grace?

This songwriter is by no means atypical. The popularity of this song is symptomatic of the lack of understanding of the term by most all of Christianity. According to the dictionary, grace is defined as unmerited favor, which basically says that it is favor that cannot be earned. We need to think of favor as being in a state of approval. If you are in someone's favor, then you are approved by them. In our human relationships, favor is almost always earned by doing or saying something, or just by being someone or something. Whether intentional or passive, that favor is earned.

If these definitions of grace and favor are true, then Christianity is in trouble, because they have been saying that only Christians can come under grace when they make covenant with Jesus. How can that be grace if you have to believe it before you get it? That is, if we believe the accepted English definition of the word grace. If we do accept the English definition, then we have to adjust our Bible interpretation accordingly.

The key to this discussion is to choose the definition that will allow the term "grace" to remain consistent with the rest of the Bible verses. Does the Bible teach that grace is given without doing anything at all, or does it teach that grace only comes to persons when they believe on Jesus?

Grace came by what Jesus did and not by your acceptance of it, for if you did something to get it, that means it was merited and not unmerited favor. You have to remember what we have found out about justification, atonement, reconciliation, etc. We have already seen in these words that it all depended on what Jesus did and had absolutely nothing to do with what you did, or did not do about it.

If we can conclude that the word "grace" in the Old Testament, originally written in Hebrew, is even remotely similar to the New Testament word "grace," we will be surprised at what we will find. Probably the most familiar Old Testament verse using the word "grace" is Genesis 6:8, "Noah found grace in the eyes of the Lord." The word should paint a picture in your mind of a superior bowing their knee to an inferior. In other words, the inferior is to be served by the superior.

"And the Word became flesh and dwelt among us, and we beheld His glory, the glory as of the only begotten of the Father, full of grace and truth." John bore witness of Him and cried out, saying, "This was He of whom I said, 'He who comes after me is preferred before me, for He was before me.' "And of His fullness we have all received, and grace for grace. For the law was given through Moses, but grace and truth came through Jesus Christ." (John 1:14-17).

We know from verse 14 that God the Father is full of grace. Then in verse 17 we see that grace come through Jesus Christ. From our other word studies we know that most everything connected with Jesus, or came about as a result of Jesus, resulted from what He did at the cross. So, we can probably be safe in saying that grace came as a result of Jesus' death on the cross, His burial and resurrection.

"But now the righteousness of God apart from the law is revealed, being witnessed by the Law and the Prophets, even the righteousness of God which is through the faith of Jesus Christ to all and on all who believe, for there is no difference; for all have sinned and fallen short of the glory of God, being justified freely by His grace through the redemption that is in Christ Jesus..." (Romans 3:21-24) We see that verse 24 tells us that all, and all who believe (v.22) are justified freely by grace. Since we have already seen that justification came by way of Jesus' blood, then we can conclude that Jesus' blood and grace are very closely related, if not synonymous.

"Now to him who works, the wages are not counted as grace, but as debt." (Romans 4:4) A short, but very profound verse, which in actuality, is the definition of grace. An employer is in debt to an employee for services rendered by the employee. If an employee receives wages or gifts without having performed a service it is then grace and not debt. It appears that we are finding out that grace does not come by way of a person's acceptance of Jesus, but, as I put forth earlier, actually comes as a free gift.

We see in Romans 4:16 that Abraham's faith and the promise are connected to grace. "For the promise that he would be the heir of the world was not to Abraham or his seed through the law, but through the righteousness of faith. For if those who are of the law are heirs, faith is made void and the promise made of no effect because the law brings about wrath; for where there is no law there is no transgression. Therefore, it is of faith that it might be according to grace, so that the promise might be sure to all the seed, not only to those who are of the law, but also to those who are of the faith of Abraham, who is the father of us all..." (Romans 4:13-16) Keep in mind that when Paul talked about faith, he often was speaking of the faith of Jesus. "Therefore, having been justified by faith, we have peace with God through our Lord Jesus Christ, through whom also we have access by faith into this grace in which we stand, and rejoice in hope of the glory of God." (Romans 5:1-2)

It says that we have not only been justified by faith, but also we have access by faith into this grace in which we stand. Paul did not say that we had access into grace by our faith. It may infer that, but it certainly does not say it. It could be that it was someone else's faith by which we have access into grace. It is just as easy to conclude that, as it is to conclude that it was our faith that attained that status.

Remember earlier how we determined that in Romans Chapter 5 the free gift is synonymous with justification brought about by Jesus' blood, we find also that grace fits into that picture. "But the free gift is not like the offense. For if by the one man's offense many died, much more the grace of God and the gift by the grace of the one Man, Jesus Christ, abounded to many. And the gift is not like that which came through the one who sinned. For the judgment which came from one offense resulted in condemnation, but the free gift which came from many offenses resulted in justification. For if by one man's offense death reigned through the one, much more those who receive abundance of grace and the gift of righteousness will reign in life through the one Jesus Christ." (Romans 5:10-17)

You will notice this last verse specifically says that the result of a person's acceptance of this grace is that they will reign in life. It does not say, nor does it imply, that if a person receives this grace they will escape eternal damnation. There is no mention of this at all. The only result of a person receiving God's grace is that they will reign in life. [That they will be above and not beneath, that they will be the head and not the tail.]

It would be enough to conclude our argument on grace at this time. However, until we look at what else the Bible says about grace, we will not be sure that what we have learned so far, is without question what Christians should teach on grace.

Romans Chapter 5 goes on to say,

"Moreover the law entered that the offense might abound. But where sin abounded, grace abounded much more, so that as sin reigned in death, even so grace might reign through righteousness to eternal life through Jesus Christ our Lord. What shall we say then? Shall we continue in sin that grace may abound?" (Romans 5:20-6:1) [Another indication that grace came about as a result of the righteousness of Jesus.] "For sin shall not have dominion over you, for you are not under law but under grace? What then? Shall we sin because we are not under law but under grace? Certainly not!"

"I say then, has God cast away His people? Certainly not!... Even so then, at this present time there is a remnant according to the election of grace. And if by grace, then it is no longer works; otherwise grace is no longer grace. But, if it is of works, it is no longer grace; otherwise work is no longer work." (Romans 11:1&15-16) [Some more evidence that if you do something to get something then it was not grace, or unmerited favor, but rather, it is considered work.]

We find in I Corinthians 1:4 again that grace came by what Jesus did. "I thank my God always concerning you for the grace of God which was given to you by Jesus Christ." Possibly, you want to interpret this verse to read that you do not receive the grace of God until you receive Jesus. Admittedly, this verse could be interpreted that way because it reads that the grace was given to you by Jesus Christ, your covenant partner: potentially, a logical interpretation. However, that interpretation does not line up with the other verses we have looked at on grace, therefore making it an invalid interpretation, unless of course, we find other verses that back up this interpretation. If we do, then we have a dilemma that needs to be resolved.

"For you know the grace of our Lord Jesus Christ, that though He was rich, yet though for your sakes He became poor, that you through his poverty might become rich." (II Corinthians 8:9) "And God is able to make all grace abound toward you, that you, always having all sufficiency in all things, have an abundance for every good work." (II Corinthians 9:8)

"I have been crucified with Christ, it is no longer I who live, but Christ lives in me; and the life which I now live in the flesh I live by the faith of the Son of God, who loved me and gave Himself for me. I do not set aside the grace of God; for if righteousness comes through the law, then Christ died in vain." (Galatians 2:20-21)

"You have become estranged from Christ, you who attempt to be justified by law; you have fallen from grace." (Galatians 5:4) [The term "fallen from grace" in no way implies the unforgiveness of God, as some preachers have portrayed it to mean. It only means that you are not resting in grace, if you are trying to work your way into God's favor.]

"To the praise of the glory of His grace, by which He has made us accepted in the beloved. In Him we have redemption through His blood, the forgiveness of sins, according to the riches of His grace which He has made to abound toward us in all wisdom and prudence, having made known to us the mystery of His will, according to His good pleasure which He purposed in Himself, that in the dispensation of the fullness of the times He might gather together in one all things in Christ, both which are in heaven and which are on earth, in Him." (Ephesians 1:6-10)

"But God, who is rich in mercy, because of His great love with which He loved us, even when we were dead in trespasses, made us alive together with Christ (by grace you have been saved), and raised us up together, and made us sit together in the heavenly places in Christ Jesus, that in the ages to come He might show the exceeding riches of His grace in His kindness toward us in Christ Jesus. For by grace you have been saved through faith, and that not of yourselves, it is the gift of God, not of works lest any man should boast." (Ephesians 2:4-9)

"For this reason I, Paul, the prisoner of Jesus Christ for you Gentiles - if indeed you have heard of the dispensation of the grace of God which was given to me for you." (Ephesians 3:1-2)

This verse is used most often to preach a dispensational theology that states that God deals with mankind according to dispensations, or periods of time. What they fail to realize is that each of their so-called dispensations began with a covenant.

"But to each one of us grace was given according to the measure of Christ's gift." (Ephesians 4:7) Now may our Lord Jesus Christ Himself, and our God and Father, who has loved us and given us everlasting consolation and good hope by grace, comfort your hearts and establish you in every good word and work." (II Thessalonians 2:16-17)

"Therefore do not be ashamed of the testimony of our Lord, nor of me His prisoner, but share with me in the sufferings for the gospel according to the power of God, who has saved us and called us with a holy calling, not according to our works, but according to His own purpose and grace which was given to us in Christ Jesus before time began." (II Timothy 1:8-9)

"For the grace of God that brings salvation has appeared to all men." (Titus 2:11) [It was the grace of God that brought salvation, not the acceptance of the grace. Also in Titus 3:7, we read,] "that having been justified by His grace we should become heirs according to the hope of eternal life."

"But we see Jesus, who was made a little lower than the angels, for the suffering of death crowned with glory and honor, that He, by the grace of God, might taste death for everyone." (Hebrews 2:9) [Here we see that it was by the grace of God that Jesus tasted death for everyone.] "Let us therefore come boldly before the throne of grace, that we may obtain mercy and find grace to help in time of need." (Hebrews 4:16)

We find two verses in Hebrews that also appear to be somewhat inconsistent with what we have said previously in this chapter.

"Of how much worse punishment, do you suppose, will he be thought worthy who has trampled the Son of God underfoot, counted the blood of the covenant by which he was sanctified a common thing and insulted the Spirit of grace?" (Hebrews 10:29) "Pursue peace with all men, and holiness, without which no one will see the Lord: looking diligently lest anyone fall short of the grace of God; lest any root of bitterness springing up cause trouble, and by this many become defiled." (Hebrews 12:14-15)

105

On the surface, it appears that these verses agree with an eternal damnation theology, but you have to keep in mind that these verses must remain consistent with the other verses we have looked at dealing with God's grace. Also, we need to keep in mind that we have to understand covenants and covenant breakers before we form our interpretations.

> "Of this salvation the prophets have inquired and searched diligently, who prophesied of the grace that would come to you, searching what, or what manner of time, the Spirit of Christ who was in them was indicating when He testified beforehand the sufferings of Christ and the glories that would follow... Therefore gird up the loins of your mind, be sober, and rest your hope fully upon the grace that is to be brought to you at the revelation of Jesus Christ." (I Peter 1:10,11,13)

> "But may the God of all grace, who called us to His eternal glory by Christ Jesus, after you have suffered awhile, perfect, establish, strengthen, and settle you." (I Peter 5:10) "By Silvanus, our faithful brother as I consider him, I have written to you briefly, exhorting and testifying that this is the true grace of God in which you stand." (I Peter 5:12)

> "For certain men have crept in unnoticed, who long ago were marked out for this condemnation, ungodly men, who turn the grace of our God into licentiousness and deny the only Lord God and our Lord Jesus Christ." (Jude 4)

We have looked at what the New Testament really says about God's grace, and, based on the accepted definition of grace, we have found that the Bible does not say what evangelical Christianity says it says. Before you forget what you have read, or, before someone attempts to talk you out of believing what you have read, I want to review the major points we have made.

(1) Grace is unmerited favor. You cannot do anything to earn it. It is given by God just because he feels like it. (2) The definition of grace suggests a superior serving an inferior. (3) Romans Chapter 3 tells us that we are justified [declared not guilty] freely by God's grace [unmerited favor]. (4) Grace came by way of the faith of Abraham. (5) Our access into grace did not come by our faith, but by the faith of Jesus. Not one place does it say that grace came by our faith. (6) Our acceptance of grace will allow us to reign in life, but it does not gain our forgiveness. (8) The dispensation of grace began with Jesus's blood being shed, therefore it began by a covenant being made. (9) Only a few verses remotely suggest that a lack of acceptance of grace will end in eternal damnation, whereas, all the other verses make it clear that grace came by what Jesus did, therefore alleviating the possibility that we could change it.

Although a beautiful song, "Amazing Grace" is not biblically accurate in its description of grace. This demonstrates once again the need to be sure that what we are saying and singing has been evaluated so that it lines up with what the Bible really says.

10

FAITH, WHO'S FAITH?

The subject of faith has really been one of the most confusing points for all of Christianity. We need to find out exactly what the Bible says about faith: whose faith, why faith, when faith, what faith? We need to look at what the Bible says about Jesus' faith. Then, there are other people's faith. We are also going to look at those people and what it was that their faith did for them. Earlier we talked about justification, that a person is justified by faith. But whose faith justifies? This question also needs to be answered. First, we need to see what the Bible says about Jesus' faith.

"But now the righteousness of God apart from the law is revealed, being witnessed by the Law and the Prophets. Even the righteousness of God which is through the faith of Jesus Christ to all and on all who believe. For there is no difference; for all have sinned and fallen short of the glory of God, being justified freely by His grace through the redemption that is in Christ Jesus," (Romans 3:21-24).

It says that the righteousness of God was through the faith of Jesus Christ to all and on all who believe, for there is no difference. There is no difference between the "all," and the "all who believe." This verse is very similar to I John 2:2, which said that Jesus paid the price for the sins of all the world. He was made the expiation for the sins of all the world. This verse said that God did it to all, and to all who believe, because there is no difference between the two categories.

Let's look at some other things about faith. Romans 3:25-26, "Whom God set forth to be an [expiation] by His blood through faith to demonstrate His righteousness because in His forbearance God had passed over the sins that were previously committed to demonstrate at the present time His righteousness, that He might be just and the justifier of the one who has faith in Jesus."

Verses 27-28, "Where is boasting then? It is excluded. By what law? Of works? No, but by the law of faith. Therefore, we conclude that a man is justified by faith, apart from the deeds of the law. Or is He the God of the Jews only? Is He not also the God of the Gentiles? Yes, of the Gentiles also, since there is one God who would justify the circumcised by faith and the uncircumcised through faith. Do we then make void the law through faith? Certainly not! On the contrary, we establish the law."

Another reference on faith is Galatians 2:16: "Knowing that a man is not justified by the works of the law but by the faith of Jesus Christ, even we have believed in Jesus Christ, that we might be justified by the faith of Christ and not by the works of the law; for by the works of the law no flesh shall be justified." This verse makes it obvious that it was by the faith of Jesus that we were declared not guilty.

Galatians 2:20 says, "I have been crucified with Christ; it is no longer I who live, but Christ lives in me; and the life which I now live in the flesh I live by the faith of the Son of God who loved me and gave Himself for me." The New King James Version says, "And the life which I now live in the flesh I live by faith in the Son of God." They totally changed the meaning of the verse by changing these two underlined words.

"But the scripture has confined all under sin that the promise by the faith of Jesus Christ might be given to those who believe." Galatians 3:22 [This verse says it is given to those who believe, but it does not say the promise will not be given to those who do not believe.]

"But before faith came, we were kept under guard by the law, kept for the faith which would afterward be revealed. Therefore, the law was our tutor to bring us to Christ, that we might be justified by faith. But after faith has come, we are no longer under a tutor." [Galatians: 23-25]. It appears here, that faith had already come. Faith was a past tense not a future tense. Whereas, the Protestant view is that faith is a future tense. When you believe, when you have faith in Jesus, then you are justified. Not so! This section says, "That we might be justified by faith, but after faith has come, we are no longer under a tutor." Meaning, faith has already come by the time the book of Galatians was written.

Also, in Ephesians 3:12, we see that the faith of Jesus is involved, starting with verse 11. "According to the eternal purpose which He accomplished in Christ Jesus our Lord, in whom we have boldness and access with some confidence through the faith of Him [Jesus]." We see again that your boldness and access with confidence came through the faith of Jesus, not through your own faith.

How does the Bible say that righteousness comes? "And be found in Him not having my own righteousness, which is from the law, but that which is through the faith of Christ, the righteousness which is from God by faith." [Philippians 3:9] "By faith," meaning Jesus' faith. Your righteousness does not come by what you do, but rather, by what Jesus did for you.

While studying the Bible, we see a couple of "faith" chapters, one of which is Galatians Chapter 3. I want to go through a large part of this.

> O foolish Galatians! Who has bewitched you that you should not obey the truth, before whose eyes Jesus Christ was clearly portrayed among you as crucified? This only, I want to learn from you. Did you receive the Spirit by the works of the law or by the hearing of faith? Are you so foolish? Having begun in the Spirit are you now being made perfect by the flesh? Have you suffered so many things in vain--if indeed it was in vain?

> Therefore, He who supplies the Spirit to you and works miracles among you does He do it by the works of the law or by the hearing of faith? --just as Abraham believed God and it was accounted to him for righteousness. Therefore, know that only those who are of faith are sons of Abraham and the scripture foreseeing that God would justify the nations by faith preached the gospel to Abraham beforehand saying, "In you all the nations shall be blessed." So then those who are of faith are blessed with believing Abraham.

> For as many as are of the works of the law are under the curse; for it is written. cursed is everyone who does not continue in all things which are written in the book of the law, to do them. But that no one is justified by the law in the sight of God is evident for "the just shall live by faith. Yet the law is not of faith, but "the man who does them shall live in them." Christ has redeemed us from the curse of the law having become a curse for us (for it is written, "cursed is everyone who hangs on a tree"), that the blessings of Abraham might come upon the Gentiles in Christ Jesus that we might receive the promise of the Spirit through faith.

The chapter talks so much about faith but, it does not really talk about whose faith it is. It does not say that it is a person's faith individually. It talks about more of a general faith. Take for instance verse 2, "this only I want to learn from you: did you receive the Spirit by the hearing of faith." Well, whose faith was it? If it is true that their justification, or their reception of the Spirit, came by their own faith, then whose faith did they hear? You cannot hear your own faith. After it is an accomplished fact, you can hear your own faith. But, this is before their faith was a fact, a point in time when their faith came into play. Well, whose faith was it?

There is another verse that goes right along with that reasoning. Verse 5 says, "Therefore, He who supplies the Spirit to you and works miracles among you, does He do it by the works of the law, or by the hearing of faith?" What faith does God hear when He performs miracles? It is not our own. It is the faith of Jesus as I have been pointing out. When people like T. L. Osborne and other missionaries go into other countries, if they are having miracles in their services just because the gospel is being preached, it is because they are preaching about the faith of Jesus. They are telling the people that believing on Jesus is what people need to do. But, God is working miracles among the people without them ever believing anything. It is just happening because the person preaching is speaking faith and they are speaking the faith of Jesus, not the faith of the individual. That is what God acts upon.

There are situations where people are basically healed by their own faith. Just reading through the gospels will tell you that, but, what I am talking about here, are those who are hearing faith. Like Galatians 3:2 says, "This only I want to learn from you: Did you receive the Spirit by the works of the law, or by the hearing of faith?" It is the hearing of Jesus' faith, that can bring your healing. When you are set free from your sins, by believing on Jesus, it is your own faith; which is a totally different subject.

We need to separate what Jesus' faith accomplished and what our faith accomplishes. Galatians 3:5 goes along with Galatians 3:2, "Therefore, He who supplies the Spirit to you and works miracles among you, does He do it by the works of the law, or by the hearing of faith?" Then we have Romans 10:8, "But what does it say? The word is near you, even in your mouth and in your heart" (That is, the word of faith which we preach)..." The word of faith that is preached is the word of what Jesus did for us, not what we do on our own.

A very important faith chapter is Hebrews Chapter 11, "Now faith is the substance of things hoped for, the evidence of things not seen." Verse 3 "By faith you will understand that the worlds were framed by the Word of God so that the things which are seen were not made of things which are visible."

"By faith Abel offered God a more acceptable sacrifice than Cain, by faith Enoch was translated so he did not see death, but without faith it is impossible to please Him for he who comes to God must believe that He is, and that He is the rewarder of those who diligently seek Him." (Hebrews 11:4) "By faith Noah being divinely warned of things not yet seen moved with Godly fear." (vs.7) "By faith Abraham obeyed when he was called to go to a place which he would afterward receive as an inheritance." (vs.8) "By faith he sojourned in the land of promise as in a foreign country," (vs.9) "By faith Sarah herself also received strength to conceive seed, and she bore a child," (vs.11); "These all died in faith not having received the promise." (vs.13) "By faith Abraham" (vs.17); "By faith Isaac blessed Jacob and Esau," (vs.20); "By faith Jacob blessed each of the sons of Joseph," (vs.21); "By faith Joseph,"(vs.22); "By faith Moses," (vs.23); "By faith Moses, again," (vs.24): "By faith they passed through the Red Sea as by dry land," (vs.29); "By faith the harlot Rahab did not perish with those who did not believe," (vs.31); "Gideon, Samson, David, Samuel, and the Prophets" (vs.32) who through faith subdued kingdoms, worked righteousness, obtained promises, stopped the mouths of lions, quenched the violence of fire, escaped the edge of the sword, out of weakness were made strong, became valiant in battle, turned to flight the armies of the aliens." Going on down to verse 39 we see: "And all these, having obtained a good testimony through faith, did not receive the promise, God having provided something better for us that they should not be made perfect apart from us."

Chapter 12, verse 1, "Therefore, we also, since we are surrounded by so great a cloud of witnesses, let us lay aside every weight and the sin which so easily ensnares us, and let us run with endurance the race that is set before us, looking unto Jesus, the author and finisher of faith, who for the joy that was set before Him endured the cross, despising the shame, and has sat down at the right hand of the throne of God."

You notice that in verse 2, I quoted it as saying, "looking unto Jesus, the author and finisher of faith." I left out the word "our" because that three-letter word has brought misunderstanding to some of us because it was put in by the translators. The translators put that word in because they had not figured out about Jesus' faith. The verse should read "looking unto Jesus, the author and finisher of faith." All these people that I mentioned earlier from Chapter 11 of Hebrews were looking forward to this faith that Jesus was talking about - what Jesus accomplished.

To verify the correct translation of that verse stating that Jesus was the author and finisher of faith, we need to go back to Galatians Chapter 3 and look at it this way. Galatians 3:22, "But the scripture has confined all under sin, that the promise by the faith of Jesus Christ might be given to those who believe. But before faith came, [notice faith in the past tense] we were kept under guard by the law, kept for the faith which would afterward be revealed. [So the faith would come later, after the law.] "Therefore, the law was our tutor to bring us to Christ, that we might be justified by faith. But after faith has come, we are no longer under a tutor."

Verse 25 is consistent with Hebrews 12:2 that Jesus was the author and finisher of faith and verse 25 says "after faith has come." It is explicit that the faith came at a certain point in time. The faith that we have been talking about here, the faith that God had Paul write about in all these letters to the different churches, was the faith of Jesus. We are justified by Jesus' faith. By the hearing of faith do the miracles come about. The preaching of faith causes things to happen. But, the justification came by what Jesus did, and not by anything that we did. It was not by our faith.

Then where does *our faith* come in? Obviously, it does not get us forgiven of our sins. Jesus's faith did that. What it does is get us released from our sins, not released from the punishment of sins. There is a big difference.

It is fairly common theology that Adam and Eve were initially in spiritual oneness with God, until they transgressed a law of their covenant [became covenant breakers]. They then became separated from God spiritually, which caused them to have an emptiness inside them, that had been filled by God's spirit in them. Keep in mind that God also had an emptiness in Him because of the separation, so He took the initiative to propose a way by which He could get mankind back into spiritual oneness with Himself.

Probably where most of Christianity has missed the understanding of Adam and Eve is that we never realized that they were in a covenant relationship with God, which brought with it certain rules and obligations. They had the blessings of the covenant as long as they obeyed the laws of the covenant. The curse of the covenant did not come into effect until the covenant was violated. The curse was obviously spiritual separation for Adam and Eve and for their descendants. We know this because the spirit is in the blood and the blood is passed on to the children.

This is all leading to the clear understanding of mankind's standing with God. The sin of the parents had passed down to the children, but not the punishment of the sin. In most every Bible covenant, when broken, the curse is visited on the children, as is true with the Adamic covenant. However, the punishment of the sin of Adam and Eve does not pass to the children, only the curse of the sin.

If God, immediately after the "fall," had intended to punish the sinner He probably would have announced it at that time. But, what do we find Him doing? We find Him announcing that He was making a new covenant with mankind [Eve]. He is the one that initiated the covenant. If He had been seeking to eternally punish all of mankind, would He not have at least given them an indication of the impending doom? It was not until hundreds of years later that a hint of eternal doom is evident.

Our subject in this chapter is faith, but to understand faith we have to see what comes with our faith, and we are only sure of that when we know what the curse of the Adamic covenant did. We have already mentioned that all of mankind, excluding Jesus, was born with a spirit that was spiritually separated from God. In order to come into a state of spiritual oneness with God, mankind had to get uncorrupted blood. This, according to all of history, could only be done by making a blood covenant with a person with uncorrupted blood. With the blood covenant comes new life [spirit], or a re-birth. That is what it means to be born-again. It means getting a new spirit inside that replaces the old, separated spirit.

History proves that Jesus was the only human being born with uncorrupted blood, meaning that no one is able to be born again without making a covenant with Jesus. Being born-again, not only gets a person into spiritual oneness with the Creator of the universe, but also gives a person access to everything that Jesus possesses. This custom is similar to our marriage covenant in its purest form.

This custom is also the proof that Jesus was the only person born with a spirit in spiritual oneness with God. We know this because people in covenant with Jesus have access to His authority [i.e., power of attorney], to get what they need or desire. This cannot be done by using the authority of anyone else who ever lived. [Note, I earlier said born, not created.] In no other name, [authority] can a person be healed, raised from the dead, or delivered from demonic possession.

This is what our faith gets us. When we have faith in Jesus, we "give [ourselves] up to Him, [we] take [ourselves] out of [our] own keeping and entrust [ourselves] into His keeping," (Acts 16:31, quoted from The Amplified Bible). That is the best description I could find to define what having faith in Jesus means. Having faith in, believing in, and making covenant with, all have the same meaning for us. Hopefully, you are able to see how important the understanding of this is to our interpretation of the Bible.

Our faith in Jesus gains us release from the sin-nature [spirit] within us, but it does not obtain our forgiveness from God. Our faith in Jesus gives us access to everything that Jesus possesses, so that we can reign in this life (Romans 5:17), on the earth (Revelations 5:10), but it does not insulate us from attacks by the enemy.

Our faith in Jesus gives us authority over the enemy but does not guarantee that the attacks will not return. Our faith in Jesus brings us that freedom for which every cell in our body cries out, but along with the freedom, comes the responsibilities of a covenant relationship. Our faith in Jesus gives us the right to ask for [demand] God's Holy Spirit to live inside us to lead and guide us twenty-four hours each and every day. So that we will no longer allow someone else to tell us what God has for us. Our faith in Jesus gets for us the greatest life we could find anywhere.

11

REPENT, OR PERISH!

The next several pages will be dedicated to covering all of the verses in the Bible that people use as their evidence for eternal damnation. However, each verse must be followed very closely to find out if that is exactly what it says. With each verse we need to ask the question, "Does it specifically say that a person will suffer eternal separation from God, or does it only possibly suggest eternal separation? By the time we are done with this section, it should be obvious which side of the argument has the most evidence.

One thing we need to cover before we look at these verses is the issue of the word "hell." In the Greek language, from which the majority of the New Testament was translated, we will find the word "hell" is translated from three different Greek words. It sometimes refers to a grave, or pit, with *hades* being the Greek word. *Hades* is roughly similar to the Hebrew word, *sheol*, which means grave. Hell is also translated from the word *gehenna*, which was a ravine, or narrow valley, outside Jerusalem. *Gehenna* was basically the garbage pit outside of Jerusalem where they burned all the garbage, rubbish, sewage, bodies of criminals, animal carcasses, etc. Also, the word *tartaros* is translated hell. It designates the condition, or imprisonment, in which God has kept the angels which rebelled with Lucifer. (II Peter 2:4)

When we see the word "hell," it may, or may not,

mean eternal separation. It may mean grave, or it may mean the garbage pit, or it may mean something else. In addition to differentiating the words that are translated "hell," we must also keep in mind under which covenant the speaker, or writer, is functioning. That bit of information can make a big difference in how the verse should be understood. Since Jesus spoke almost everything from a standpoint of the Old Covenant, then what He said about hell, or punishment, may, very likely, have referred to the status of mankind under that covenant.

Matthew 5:29-30, "And if your right eye causes you to sin, pluck it out and cast it from you; for it is more profitable for you that one of your members perish, than for your whole body to be cast into hell [*gehenna*]. And if your right hand causes you to sin, cut it off and cast it from you; for it is more profitable for you that one of your members perish, than for your whole body to be cast into hell [*gehenna*].

Matthew 10:22, "And you will be hated by all for My namesake. But he who endures to the end will be saved." Matthew 13:41-42, "The Son of Man shall send out His angels, and they will gather out of His kingdom all these that offend, and those who practice lawlessness, and will cast them into the furnace of fire. There will be wailing and gnashing of teeth." [Is this Old or New Covenant?]

Matthew 18:6, "But whoever causes one of these little ones who believe in me to sin, it would be better for him if a millstone were hung around his neck and he were drowned in the depth of the sea." Matthew 18:8, "And if your hand or feet causes you to sin, cut it off and cast it from you. It is better for you to enter into life lame or maimed, rather than having two hands or two feet, to be cast into the everlasting fire. [*Gehenna?*] And if your eye causes you to sin, pluck it out and cast it from you. It is better for you to enter into life with one eye, rather than having two eyes, to be cast into hellfire." [*Gehenna*] Matthew 18:34-35, "And his master was angry, and delivered him to the torturers until he should pay all that was due to him. So My Heavenly Father also will do to you if each of you, from his heart, does not forgive his brother his trespasses."

Matthew 19:17, "So he said to him, 'Why do you call me good? No one is good but one, that is, God. But if you want to enter into life, keep the commandments.'" [Old Covenant] Matthew 23:14-15, "Woe to you, Scribes and Pharisees, hypocrites! For you devour widows' houses, and for a pretense make long prayers. Therefore, you will receive greater condemnation." [Condemnation could be translated judgment.] "Woe to you, Scribes and Pharisees, hypocrites! Because you travel land and sea to win one proselyte, and when he is won, you make him twice as much a son of hell [*Gehenna*] as yourself." Matthew 23:33, "Serpents, brood of vipers! How can you escape the condemnation of hell?" [*Gehenna*]

Matthew 24:12-13, "And because lawlessness will abound, the love of many will grow cold. But he who endures to the end shall be saved." Matthew 24:48-51, "But if that evil servant says in his heart, 'My master is delaying his coming,' and begins to beat his fellow servants, and to eat and drink with the drunkards, the master of that servant will come on a day when he is not looking for him and an hour that he is not aware of, and will cut him in two and will appoint him his portion with the hypocrites. There shall be weeping and gnashing of teeth."

You can read also chapter 25 of Matthew. It talks about the parable of the wise and foolish servants. That parable is used quite often as evidence of Jesus returning and saying that, "I do not know you." [We need to know that Hebrew parables do not necessarily mean what they may seem to mean on the surface. They do not translate easily into English.] Also, in chapter 25, we find the parable of the servants, verse 30, "And cast the unprofitable servant into the outer darkness. There will be weeping and gnashing of teeth. Verse 32, "All the nations will be gathered before Him, who will separate them one from another, as a shepherd divides his sheep from the goats." Verses 33-34, "And he will set the sheep on His right hand, but the goats on the left. And the King will say to those on His right hand, 'Come, you blessed of My Father, inherit the kingdom prepared for you from the foundation of the world:'" Verse 41, "Then He will also say to those on the left hand, 'Depart from me you cursed into the everlasting fire prepared for the Devil and his angels;'" Verse 46, "And these will go away into everlasting punishment, but the righteous into eternal life."

We find that the separation of sheep and goats has already happened, or is happening as you read this book. We know that because verse 31 says, "He will sit on the throne of His glory." Jesus did that when He came out of the tomb and was given all authority in heaven and earth. At a future point in time, Jesus will hand back to the Father all that authority and divest Himself of His glory. Therefore, we know that Jesus coming in His glory is past tense, and He is sitting on the throne at this moment. That leaves us having to interpret this chapter in the present tense and not in a future tense.

More proof of this is in verse 34, which talks about the blessed of the Father inheriting the kingdom that was prepared before the foundation of the world. This kingdom is now. The blessings can be had now by those who have a covenant relationship with the Father through Jesus. Separating the covenants and understanding the difference between the realm of heaven and the kingdom of heaven would have aided people in correct interpretation of this chapter.

Also, in verse 46, we find more proof of this being in the present tense. The righteous go into eternal life. [Eternal life is always in the present tense in the New Testament.] John 17:3, "And this is eternal life, that they may know You, the only true God, and Jesus Christ whom You have sent." Eternal life, according to this verse, comes about by having a covenant relationship with God and Jesus, which is present tense. That eternal life is inside us and is not something we will receive after the judgment.

The only verse in this whole chapter that I do not have a ready rebuttal against is verse 41. "Depart from Me, you cursed, into the everlasting fire prepared for the devil and his angels." I do know this: The only humans that are going to be eternally separated from God will be covenant breakers who have become cursed because they walked away from their covenant with God! That is the only interpretation that will keep this verse consistent with the rest of the New Testament.

In the Book of Mark, this is what we find.

Mark 8:36, "For what will it profit a man if be gains the whole world and loses his own soul?" Mark 9:42-48, [See Mt. 5:29-30]; Mark 10:15, "Assuredly, I say to you, whoever has not received the Kingdom of God as a little child will by no means enter it." [Enter the Kingdom, not necessarily the realm.] Mark 13:27, "And then he will send His angels and gather together His elect from the four winds, from the farthest part of the earth to the farthest part of Heaven."

Luke 3:17, "His winnowing fan is in His hand, and He will thoroughly purge His threshing floor, and gather the wheat into His barn; but the chaff He will burn with unquenchable fire." Luke 9:25-26, "For what advantage is it to a man if he gains the whole world, and is himself destroyed or lost? For whoever is ashamed of Me and My words, to him the Son of Man will be ashamed when He comes in His own glory, and in His Father's and of the holy angels." [Keep in mind the position of a covenant breaker]

Luke 10:14-15, " But it will be more tolerable for Tyre and Sidon than for you. And you, Capernaum, who are exalted to Heaven, will be thrust down to *Hades*." Luke 12:5, "But I will show you whom you should fear: Fear Him who, after He has killed, has power to cast into hell [*gehenna*]; yes, I say to you, fear Him!" Luke 12:9, "But he who denies Me before men will be denied before the angels of God." [Covenant breakers!]

Luke 12:20-21, "But God said to him, "You fool! This night your soul will be required of you; then who's will those things be which you have provided? So is he who lays up treasure for himself, and is not rich toward God." Luke 13:3 & 5, "I tell you, no; but unless you repent you will all likewise perish." [New Covenant, or Old Covenant?]

Luke 13:24-30, "Strive to enter through the narrow gate, for many, I say to you, will seek to enter and will not be able. When once the master of the house has risen up and shut the door, and you began to stand outside and knock at the door, saying, "Lord, Lord, open for us," and he will answer and say to you, "I do not know you, where you are from," then you will begin to say, "We ate and drunk in your presence and you taught in our streets." But he will say, "I tell you I do not know you, where you are from. Depart from me all you workers of iniquity. There will be weeping and gnashing of teeth, when you see Abraham and Isaac and Jacob and all the prophets in the Kingdom of God, and yourselves thrust out. They will come from the east and the west, from the north and south, and sit down in the Kingdom of God. And indeed there are last who will be first, and there are first who will be last."

Luke 14:27, "And whoever does not bear his cross and come after Me cannot be My disciple." Luke 15:21, "And the son said to him, "Father, I have sinned against Heaven and in your sight, and am no longer worthy to be called your son."

In chapter 16 of Luke, you will find the story of the rich man and Lazarus. Of my entire discussion, this is the weakest link for me, and on the surface, the strongest for eternal damnation theology. However, it must be studied in its Hebrew setting before any conclusions can be made. Unfortunately, most preachers have never studied it as a Hebrew idiom, therefore they teach that it means something totally different than it may actually mean. You know it well enough, so I will not cover it here.

Luke 17:2, "It will be better for him if a millstone were hung around his neck and he were thrown into the sea, than that he should offend one of these little ones." [A lot of people have gotten excited about Luke 17:20-37, where it talks about the coming of the Kingdom of God, but there you have no evidence whatsoever when you understand the difference between the Kingdom and the realm of Heaven.]

Luke 18:25, "For it is easier for a camel to go through a needle's eye, than for a rich man to enter the Kingdom of God." Luke 20:35-36, "But those who are counted worthy to obtain that age and the resurrection from the dead neither marry, nor are given in marriage; nor can they die anymore, for they are equal to the angels and are sons of God, being sons of the resurrection."

John 3:3, "Jesus answered and said to him, "Most assuredly, I say to you, unless one is born again, he can not [perceive] the Kingdom of God." John 3:5, "Jesus answered, "Most assuredly, I say to you, unless one is born of water and the spirit, he can not enter the Kingdom of God."

John 3:14-19, "And as Moses lifted up the serpent in the wilderness, even so must the Son of Man be lifted up, that whoever believes in Him shall not perish but have eternal life. For God so loved the world that He gave His only begotten Son, that whoever believes in Him shall not perish, but have everlasting life. For God did not send His Son into the world to condemn the world, but that the world through Him might be saved. [It says that *the world would not be condemned.*]

Verse 18, "He who believes in Him is not condemned; but he who does not believe is condemned already, because he has not believed in the name of the only begotten Son of God, and this is the condemnation, that the Light has come into the world, and men love darkness rather than light, because their deeds were evil." [Keep in mind the word condemned can be translated judgment.] John 3:36, "He who believes in the Son has everlasting life; and he who does not believe the Son shall not see life, but the wrath of God abides on him."

John 5:24, "Most assuredly, I say to you, he who hears My word, and believes in Him who sent Me, has everlasting life, shall not come into judgment, but has passed from death into life." John 5:36, "But I have greater witness than John's; for the works which the Father has given Me to finish--the very works that I do--bear witness of Me, that the Father has sent Me." John 6:27, "Do not labor for the food which perishes, but for the food which endures to eternal life, which the Son of Man will give you, because God the Father has set His seal on Him." John 6:29, "Jesus answered and said to them, 'This is the work of God, that you believe in Him whom He sent.'"

John 6:32, "Then Jesus said to them, 'Most assuredly, I say to you Moses did not give you the bread from Heaven, but My Father gives you the true bread from Heaven.'" Verse 35, "And Jesus said to them, "I am the bread of Life. He who comes to Me shall never hunger, and he who believes in Me shall never thirst.'"

John 8:24, "Therefore I said to you that you will die in your sins; for if you do not believe that I am He, you will die in your sins." John 8:44, "You are of your father the Devil, and the desires of your father you want to do. He was a murderer from the beginning, and does not stand in the truth, because there is no truth in Him. When he speaks a lie, he speaks from his own resources, for he is a liar and the father of it." Verse 47, "He who is of God hears God's words; therefore you do not hear, because you are not of God."

John 9:31, "Now we know that God does not hear sinners; but if anyone is a worshiper of God, and does His will, He hears him." John 15:6, "If anyone does not abide in Me, he is cast out as a branch and is withered; and they gather them and throw them into the fire, and they are burned." John 15:22, "If I had not come and spoken to them, they would have no sin, but now they have no excuse for their sin." Acts 16:31, "So they said, 'Believe on the Lord Jesus Christ, and you will be saved, you and your household.'"

Romans 1:16-19, "For I am not ashamed of the gospel of Christ, for it is the power of God to salvation for everyone who believes, for the Jew first and also for the Greek. For in it the righteousness of God is revealed from faith to faith; as it is written, 'The just shall live by faith.' For the wrath of God is revealed from Heaven against all ungodliness and unrighteousness of men, who suppress the truth in unrighteousness because what may be known of God is manifest in them for God has shown it to them."

Romans 1:28-32, "And even if they did not like to retain God in their knowledge, God gave them over to a debased mind, to do those things which are not fitting; being filled with all unrighteousness, sexual immorality, wickedness, covetousness, maliciousness; full of envy, murder, strife, deceit, evil-mindedness; they are whisperers, backbiters, haters of God, violent, proud, boasters, inventors of evil things, disobedient to parents, undiscerning, untrustworthy, unloving, unforgiving, unmerciful; who knowing the righteous judgment of God, that those who practice such things are worthy of death, not only do the same but always approve of those who practice them."

Romans 2:8-9, "But to those who are self seeking and do not obey the truth, but obey unrighteousness, indignation and wrath, tribulation and anguish, on every soul of man who does evil, of the Jew first and also of the Greek;" Romans 3:16, "Destruction and misery is in their ways; and the way of peace they have not known." There is no fear of God before their eyes." Romans 3:26, "To demonstrate at the present time His righteousness, that He might be just, and the justifier of the one who has faith in Jesus." [A true statement, but not a statement of truth.]

Romans 6:16-17, "Do you not know that to whom you present yourselves slaves to obey, you are that one's slave whom you obey, whether of sin to death [separation], or of obedience to righteousness? But God be thanked that though you were slaves of sin, yet you obeyed from the heart that form of doctrine to which you were delivered."

Romans 6:21-23, "What fruit did you have then in

the things of which you are now ashamed for the end of those things is death [separation]. But, now having been set free from sin, and having become slaves of God, you have your fruit to holiness, and the end everlasting life. For the wages of sin is death [separation], but the gift of God is eternal life in Jesus Christ our Lord."

Romans 11:21-22, "For if God did not spare the natural branches, He may not spare you either. Therefore, consider the goodness and severity of God: On those who fall, severity; but toward you, goodness, if you continue in His goodness. Otherwise you also will be cut off." [Covenant breakers are cut off!] Romans 14:23, "But he who doubts is condemned if he eats, because he does not eat from faith; for whatever is not from faith is sin."

I Corinthians 1:8, "Who will also confirm you to the end, that you may be blameless in the day of our Lord Jesus Christ." I Corinthians 1:18, "For the message of the cross is foolishness to those who are perishing, but to us who are being saved it is the power of God." I Corinthians 1:21, "For since, in the wisdom of God, the world through wisdom did not know God, it pleased God through the foolishness of the message preached to save those who believe."

I Corinthians 6:9-11, "Do you not know that the unrighteous will not inherit the Kingdom of God? Do not be deceived. Neither fornicators, nor adulterers, nor homosexuals, nor sodomites, nor thieves, nor coveters, nor drunkards, nor revilers, nor extortioners will inherit the Kingdom of God. And such were some of you. But you were washed, but you were sanctified, but you were justified in the name of the Lord Jesus and by the spirit of our God."

I Corinthians 15:2, "By which also you are saved, if you hold fast that word which I preached to you--unless you believed in vain." I Corinthians

15:17-18, "And if Christ is not risen, your faith is futile; you are still in your sins! Then also those who have fallen asleep in Christ have perished." I Corinthians 15:30, "And why do we stand in jeopardy every hour?"

Galatians 3:22, "But the scripture has confined all under sin, that the promise by the faith of Jesus might be given to those who believe." Galatians 5:19-21, "Now the works of the flesh are evident, which are: adultery, fornication, uncleanness, licentiousness, idolatry, sorcery, hatred, contentions, jealousies, outbursts of wrath, selfish ambitions, dissensions, heresies, envy, murders, drunkenness, revelries, and the like; of which I tell you beforehand, just as I also told you in times past, that those who practice such things will not inherit the Kingdom of God." [When is the Kingdom of God?]

Ephesians 5:5, "For this you know, no fornicator, unclean person, nor covetous man, who is an idolater, has any inheritance in the kingdom of Christ and God." Verse 6, "Let no one deceive you with empty words, for because of these things the wrath of God comes upon the sons of disobedience."

Philippians 3:18-19, "For many walk, of whom I have told you often, now I tell you even weeping, that they are the enemies of the cross of Christ: Whose end is destruction, whose God is their belly, and whose glory is in their shame-who set their mind on earthly things." Colossians 1:23, "If indeed you continue in the faith, grounded and steadfast, and are not moved away from the hope of the gospel which you heard, which was preached to every creature under Heaven, of which I, Paul, became a minister." [Speaking of covenant breakers again.]

I Thessalonians 4:14, "For if we believe that Jesus died and rose again, even so God will bring with him those who sleep in Jesus." II Thessalonians

1:8-10, "In flaming fire taking vengeance on those who do not know God, and on those who do not obey the gospel of our Lord Jesus Christ. These shall be punished with everlasting destruction from the presence of the Lord and from the glory of His power, when He comes, in that day, to be glorified in the saints and to be admired by all those who believe, because our testimony among you was believed."

I Timothy 5:15, "For some who have already turned aside after Satan." [Covenant breakers.] I Timothy 5:24, "Some men's sins are clearly evident, proceeding them to judgment, but those of some men follow later." II Timothy 2:10-12, "Therefore, I endure all things for the sake of the elect, that they also may obtain the salvation which is in Christ Jesus with eternal glory. This is a faithful saying: For if we died with Him, we shall also live with Him. If we endure, we shall also reign with Him. If we deny Him, He also will deny us."

II Timothy 3:6-7, "For of this sort are those who creep into households and make captives of gullible women loaded down with sins, led away by various lusts, always learning and never able to come to the knowledge of the truth." II Timothy 4:8, "Finally, there is laid up for me the crown of righteousness, which the Lord, the righteous judge, will give to me on that day, not to me only but also to all who have loved His appearing."

Hebrews 3:14-15, "For we have became partakers of Christ if we hold the beginning of our confidence steadfast to the end, while it is said: 'Today, if you will hear His voice, do not harden your hearts as in the rebellion.'" Hebrews 5:9, "And having been perfected, He became the author of eternal salvation to all who obey Him," [Is He not also the author of eternal salvation for those who do not obey Him?] Hebrews 7:25, "Therefore He is also able to save to the uttermost those who come to God through Him,

133

since He ever lives to make intercession for them."

Hebrews 9:14-15, "How much more shall the blood of Christ, who through the eternal spirit offered himself without spot to God, purge your conscience from dead works to serve the living God? And for this reason He is the mediator of the new covenant, by means of death, for the redemption of the transgressions under the first covenant, that those who are called may receive the promise of the eternal inheritance."

Hebrews 10:26-31, "For if we sin willfully after we have received the knowledge of the truth, there no longer remains the sacrifice for sins, but of certain fearful expectation of judgment, and fiery indignation which will devour the adversaries. Anyone who has rejected Moses' law dies without mercy on the testimony of two or three witnesses. Of how much worse punishment, do you suppose, will he be felt worthy who has trampled the Son of God under foot, counted the blood of the covenant by which he was sanctified a common thing, and insulted the Spirit of grace? For we know Him who said, "Vengeance is mine; I will repay, says the Lord." And again, "The Lord will judge His people." It is a fearful thing to fall into the hands of the living God." [Referring to covenant-breakers again.]

Hebrews 10:38-39, "Now the just shall live by faith; but if anyone draws back, my soul has no pleasure in him.' [Covenant-breaker?] But we are not of those who draw back to perdition, but of those who believe to the saving of the soul." Hebrews 12:25, "See that you do not refuse Him who speaks. For if they do not escape who refuse Him who spoke on earth, much more shall we not escape if we turn away from Him who speaks from Heaven."

James 1:15, "Then, when desire has conceived, it

gives birth to sin; and sin, when it is full grown, brings forth death [separation]." James 2:5, "Listen, my beloved brethren: Has God not chosen the poor of this world to be rich in faith and heirs to the Kingdom which He promised to those who love Him?" [The Kingdom is now!]

James 2:9, "But if you show partiality, you commit sin and are convicted by the law as transgressors." [Old Covenant] James 4:4, "Adulterers and adulteresses! Do you not know that friendship with the world is enmity with God? Whoever therefore wants to be a friend of the world makes himself an enemy of God." James 5:19-20, "Brethren, if anyone among you wanders from the truth, and someone turns him back, let him know that he who turns a sinner from the error of his way will save a soul from death [separation] and cover a multitude of sins."

I Peter 1:9, "Receiving the end of your faith--the salvation of your souls." II Peter 2:9, "Then the Lord knows how to deliver the godly out of temptations and to reserve the unjust under punishment for the day of judgment."

I John 1:9, "If we confess our sins, He is faithful and just to forgive us our sins and to cleanse us from all unrighteousness." [Keep in mind what we said earlier about this verse, and how it was written to Christians, and not to unbelievers.]

I John 1:11, "But he who hates his brother is in darkness and walks in darkness, and does not know where he is going, because the darkness has blinded his eyes." I John 1:15, "Do not love the world or the things in the world. If anyone loves the world, the love of the Father is not in him." I John 1:17, "And the world is passing away, and the lust of it; but he who does the will of God abides forever." I John 1:22, "Who is a liar, but he who denies that Jesus is the Christ? He is anti-Christ who denies the Father and the Son. Whoever denies the Son does not have the Father either; he who acknowledges the Son has the Father also."

I John 3:6, "Whoever abides in Him does not sin, whoever sins has neither seen Him nor known Him." I John 3:10, "In this the children of God and the children of the devil are manifest: whoever does not practice righteousness is not of God, nor is he who does not *agape* his brother." I John 3:14, "We know that we have passed from death to life, because we *agape* the brethren. He who does not *agape* his brother abides in death." [We have never seen *agape*, let alone practiced it, so we must be abiding in death.]

I John 4:3, "And every spirit that does not confess that Jesus Christ has come in the flesh is not of God. And this is the spirit of the anti-Christ, which you have heard was coming, and is now already in the world." I John 4:5, "They are of the world. Therefore they speak as of the world, and the world hears them."

I John 5:1, "Whoever believes that Jesus is the Christ is born of God, and everyone who *agapes* him who begot also *agapes* him who is begotten of Him." I John 5:4-5, "For whatever is born of God overcomes the world. And this is the victory that has overcome the world--our faith. Who is he who overcomes the world, but he who believes that Jesus is the Son of God?" [We overcome the world by our faith. We do not obtain forgiveness by our faith.]

I John 5:10, "He who believes in the Son of God has the witness in himself; he who does not believe God has made Him a liar, because be has not believed the testimony that God has given of His Son." I John 5:12, "He who has the Son has life; he who does not have the Son of God does not have life." [The life is inside you now!]

Jude 5-7, "But I want to remind you, though you once knew this, that the Lord, having saved the people out of the land of Egypt, afterward destroyed those who did not believe." [Covenant-breakers] "And the angels who did not keep their proper domain, but left their own habitation, He has reserved in everlasting chains under darkness for the judgment of the great day; as Sodom and Gomorrah, and the cities around them in a similar manner to these, having given themselves over to sexual immorality and gone after strange flesh, are set forth as an example, suffering the vengeance of eternal fire."

Jude 14-15, ..."Behold, the Lord comes with ten thousands of His saints, to execute judgment on all, to convict all who are ungodly among them of all their ungodly deeds which they have committed in an ungodly way, and of all the harsh things which ungodly sinners have spoken against Him."

Revelation 2:11, "He who has an ear, let him hear what the spirit says to the churches. He who overcomes shall not be hurt by the second death." Rev. 2:26, "And he who overcomes, and keeps My works until the end, to him I will give power over the nations-- "He shall rule them with a rod of iron; as the potter's vessels shall be broke into pieces--as I also have received from My Father."

Rev. 9:4-5, "They were commanded not to harm the grass of the earth, or any green thing, or any tree, but only those men who do not have the seal of God on their foreheads. And they were not given authority to kill them, but to torment them for five months. Their torment was like the torment of a scorpion when it strikes a man." Rev. 13:8, "And all who dwell on the earth will worship him, whose names have not been written in the Book of Life of the Lamb slain from the foundation of the world." Rev. 14:9-11, "Then a third angel followed them saying with a loud voice, 'If anyone worships the

137

beast and his image, and receives his mark on his forehead or on his hand, he himself shall also drink of the wine of the wrath of God, which is poured out full strength into the cup of His indignation. And he shall be tormented with fire and brimstone in the presence of the holy angels and in the presence of the Lamb. And the smoke of their torment ascends forever and ever; and they have no rest day or night, who worship the beast and his image, and whoever receives the mark of his name.'"

Rev. 21:8, "But the cowardly, unbelieving , abominable, murders, sexually immoral, sorcerers, idolaters, and all liars shall have their part in the lake which burns with fire and brimstone, which is the second death." [There is another verse which deals with the second death when death and *Hades* are cast into the lake of fire. That is considered the second death. Which one is the second death? Or, are both the second death?]

How many of these verses specifically say that an unbeliever will be separated from God for eternity? In all honesty, we have to admit that the evidence is lacking for eternal damnation theology.

12

THE ETERNAL COVENANT

This is a subject that most Christians know nothing about, yet it is probably one of the most important subjects in the entire Bible. It is certainly the hinge on which the subject of eternal damnation pivots. If what we see in this chapter is true, then any other argument for an "eternal damnation" theology must cease. That is a pretty strong statement, but we have to see how strong this idea of blood covenant is.

For me, this was the first realization I ever had that God had nothing against mankind. When I was first confronted with this truth, I knew there was no turning back. This is similar, to the point in time, for most of us, when we decided to make Jesus, Lord of our life. We knew at that time that there was no turning back. We were going all the way, no matter what. The same is true of this subject of the eternal covenant. If you do not want to have to make that decision, then you do not want to read this chapter. It is that serious! This is the one proof of the argument against eternal damnation, that, if there is a covenant that guarantees that someone else took our punishment, then we have to accept it!

In order to understand the subject of eternal damnation, we must know what the terms of the eternal covenant were. We need to know everything about it, so we are going to start out with Hebrews 13:20. "Now the God of peace who brought again from the dead, our Lord

Jesus Christ, the great shepherd of the sheep, with the blood of the eternal covenant..." Now *we* have to stop and evaluate this covenant. What did it do? Who was involved? What are the characteristics [laws, blessings, cursings, gifts, etc.] of this covenant? How does this covenant apply to, or affect, those people who are not directly involved?

We can start out by attaching this characteristic to this, or any other covenant: Galatians 3:15, "Brethren I speak in the manner of men: though it is only a man's covenant, yet if it is confirmed, no one annuls or adds to it." We learn here that if any covenant is confirmed, or sealed, then nobody can change that particular covenant. That covenant can be amended or changed only by the parties that made the covenant, and then only by actually making a new covenant which could be just like the first covenant with any changes. Also, they still have to go through the ceremony again to make it valid.

This verse is also historically accurate when we study the history of covenants. In my study of covenants, I never found any covenant changed that was not changed by the parties that made the covenant. This is also true in the legal realm of contract law. Any changes to be made in a signed contract can only be made by the parties to the contract or their representative. Any time a contract is changed by any other person, or even, only one of the parties to the contract, then that contract [covenant] is invalid, illegal, and susceptible to a lawsuit.

We can surmise then, that if this eternal covenant spoken of in Hebrews 13:20 is, or has been confirmed, then it cannot be changed by anyone, except the parties directly involved in the covenant. So, it seems that we have to break this subject down, and get all the information that we can about this eternal covenant, then put it back together piece by piece, to get a clear understanding of what this eternal covenant really is.

140

We know from history that all blood covenants were made by the shedding of blood, whether animal or human blood, taking in of blood or a substitute for blood [wine, grape juice, salt, smoking a peace pipe, etc.]. The covenant in question is no different because it says the "blood" of the eternal covenant. So, we know there was blood connected with this covenant, but we still do not know what blood, whose blood, when the blood was shed, where the blood was shed, how it may affect us.

We do not have to ask why the blood. History tells us that a blood covenant was the most binding, sacred agreement that could be made between two or more parties. Why blood? That is simple, because from day six, man has considered blood to contain the life of a person, or animal, and therefore sacred. Why was it sacred? Because also from day six, man has believed, and taught, that the blood came from God, the giver of life. These are basic historical facts that can be verified through many sources, besides being foundational biblical teachings. Adam in Hebrew means God's blood. [You may want to digest these important principles before continuing].

Just from this one verse, what else can we put together about this covenant? We see that God brought again from the dead the Lord Jesus Christ, the great Shepherd of the sheep by the blood of that covenant. Since we know it was Jesus who was raised from the dead, an historical fact, and since His death was caused by the loss of blood, then we are probably going to conclude that Jesus had something to do with that eternal covenant. That is, unless we can find some other blood, or acceptable substitute for blood, involved in the raising of Jesus from the dead.

Investigating this last possibility, we would have to look into what, if any, blood was being shed around the time of His death, burial, and up to the seventy-two hours immediately preceding the actual moment of resurrection. From my knowledge, I do not know of any sacrifices being made at that time of year, which appears to have been during the Feast of Unleavened Bread [Exodus 12:17, Mark 14:1] other than the Passover lambs being used by the entire Hebrew nation. Nothing significant about that, whereby we can conclude that an eternal covenant had been struck. The Hebrews had been doing the same sacrificing of lambs every Passover for centuries. To my knowledge, there were no other sacrifices being offered during the Feast of Unleavened Bread, which was going on while Jesus was in the tomb.

The only other thing I can find is that the evening before the crucifixion, He ate the Passover with the disciples, the so-called Last Supper, or the Lord's Supper. It is there that He said, "This is my blood of the new covenant which is shed for many for the remission of sin." (Matthew 26:28) After all, the cup, or wine, was an acceptable substitute when cutting or making covenants. However, this wine does not seem a likely candidate for the beginning of an eternal covenant. Besides, He really was not doing anything different than any of the other Hebrews were doing on that Passover, except He was just explaining to His friends what significance the bread and wine actually had in the Passover. But, we still are not certain that Jesus' blood was the blood that was shed in cutting the eternal covenant in question.

Let us review what we know so far about this covenant. (1) Because it was a blood covenant, we know that it was a binding, sacred agreement between two or more parties representing themselves only, or possibly representing more persons than just themselves. (2) We know that the covenant will be in force until one of the parties is dead, or is unable to continue as master, or servant of the covenant, or until the covenant is broken, at which time the curse of this covenant comes into effect and the offended party is no longer under obligation to the covenant [similar to divorce]. (3) We know that there are certain requirements [laws] that each party is obligated to perform. (the non-performance of which would automatically bring the curse upon the offending party). The requirements may be different for each party. (4) We know that each party will receive specified and agreed upon blessings which also may be different for each party. (5) We also know that some type of gift giving must accompany the covenant, or else, the covenant is not considered to be confirmed [ratified or sealed]. (6) We know that once the covenant is confirmed, then the covenant remains, as agreed upon until it is broken by one of the parties, or one of the parties ceases to exist. (7) We also know that the blood of the covenant was the cause of Jesus being raised from the dead.

These characteristics of covenants we know already from history. So, it is nothing new that we have to learn, but what we do have to learn is who the parties involved were, what the requirements of each party were, and what the blessings and cursings were/are. How do we know for sure that the covenant was confirmed, and how do we know, without a doubt, it is still in effect?

Hopefully, we will be able to find the answers to all these questions in the Bible, and we will never question this covenant again. And, remember, once we find the answers to these questions about this covenant no one can add to the covenant, or take away from it.

[At this point, if you have not been able to totally grasp the characteristics of covenants, you may want to take some time to study them, so as we move on you will be able to follow without any problems.]

It is an historical fact that Jesus of Nazareth was crucified on a cross [a Roman custom] about the year 33 C.E. Sources verify this as fact. However, the sources do not totally agree upon the significance of that fact, and that is what so much of this fussing and fighting has been about these many centuries. So, the question is not if He died as recorded, but rather, what all does His death mean?

We will take this step by step so everything is perfectly clear. One of the main reasons why there has been such controversy in this area is because most people fail to first build a foundation under the subject, as I have done with our historical facts about covenants, and build on it block [verse] by block [verse]. ["Precept upon precept, line upon line..." Isaiah 28:10]

Let's start building by seeing what other pertinent information might be gathered from history, and the Bible, that will possibly shed some more light on the subject. The Apostle Paul tells us that Jesus was our Passover sacrificed for us. Now, if Paul, being a Hebrew, stated that Jesus was our Passover, then we can assume that Jesus was crucified on the day of the Passover Celebration, which is verified by studying the Gospel. Very quickly, we will review that.

Since we know that Jesus followed the law regarding feasts, if we follow closely the narrative in John 14-19, and Matthew 26, we see that the meal was eaten in the evening before the preparation day of the Passover. Having just a basic knowledge of the feasts, we know that the preparation was for the feast of Unleavened Bread, which would begin at sunset following Passover Day. Also, we know that this first day of the feast was a High Day, or an annual Sabbath, which always fell on the 15th of the first Hebrew month, regardless of the day of the week, meaning, this High Day, or Sabbath, could have been on any day of the week in question which would have given Him two Sabbaths to prepare for that week.

Jesus and friends were eating supper, it was obviously eaten on Passover evening, which would correspond to our Tuesday. Immediately after the meal, they were in the garden praying and sleeping, respectively, followed by the betrayal, trial, scourgings, crucifixion, and burial all that night and the following day, which was Passover Day, before sunset on our Wednesday. The religious leaders could not allow him to be on the cross on that Sabbath, so He had to be buried sometime before sunset on Wednesday, since we know how strict they were about the Sabbath.

Since Jesus died shortly before 3:00 p.m. [the ninth hour] that afternoon, then Joseph of Arimathea had plenty of time for the burial. Seeing He died from the loss of blood shortly before the end of Passover, there probably were not many sacrifices being made at that time, certainly not significant ones, anyway. Then during the period He was in the grave, three days and three nights, [Wed. sunset to Sat. sunset] in order to fulfill scripture, no significant sacrifices were being made.

We know from studying the Feast of Unleavened Bread in Leviticus 23:6-8, that the people were eating unleavened bread and making an offering by fire, each of the seven days of this feast. Even if these offerings were sacrificial offerings, instead of grain offerings, it would not be significant, because this custom had been observed for centuries.

So, we are fairly safe in assuming that no other blood could have been used to cut an eternal covenant. We still do not know a lot about this covenant, let alone answer the questions that must be answered about it. Basically, all we have done so far is review some familiar historical facts. I want to review what Paul meant about Jesus being our Passover sacrificed for us.

We know from studying the history of covenants

that the Passover, or "cross-over" sacrifice, was nothing new to the Hebrews in Egypt [Hebrews 12], as it was a common custom throughout the world during that period of time. It is commonly known as a "threshold covenant."

> "A covenant welcome was given to a guest who was to become as one of the family, or to a bride, or bridegroom, in marriage by the outpouring of blood on the threshold of the door and by staining the doorway itself with the blood of the covenant. And, now Jehovah announced that He was to visit Egypt on a designated night and that those who would welcome Him should prepare a threshold covenant or a Passover sacrifice, as a proof of that welcome, for where no such welcome was made ready for Him by a family, he must count the household as His enemy." *The Threshold Covenant,* by H. Clay Trumbull, p. 203-204, (out of print).

Contrary to popular opinion, on the Lord's part He did not "pass-over" the houses, but rather, according to the custom, He crossed over the bloodstained threshold and made a new covenant with them as explained by Jeremiah. "Behold the days are coming, says [Jehovah], when I will make a new covenant with the house of Israel and with the house of Judah - not according to the covenant I made with their fathers in the day that I took them by the hand to bring them out of the land of Egypt, my covenant which they broke, though I was a husband to them." (Jeremiah 31:31-34)

Note the part about the husband. It is obvious that God is sticking to the well known custom as explained above, "that the first Passover night was the night when Jehovah took to himself in covenant union the 'virgin of Israel' and became a husband to her. From that time forward, any recognition of, or affiliation with, another god is called 'whoredom,' 'adultery ,' or 'fornication.' In this light it is that the Prophets always speak of idolatry"

(Trumbull, pp. 212-213). Now, if we look at Jesus as a Passover sacrifice for us in light of the history surrounding the Passover, then we know that there was a basic marriage ceremony going on at that Passover. We know that God was to be the bridegroom, but, so far, it is unclear about the bride.

Let's look at the possibilities for the identity of the bride at this marriage. We can rule out Jesus because He was the Lamb in this instance. Paul said "us," meaning exactly who? Since he was writing to the church at Corinth, he could have been referring to just Hebrews. Since Corinth was in Greece and the church probably took in some Hellenists [Greeks], and if the "us" included even a few Greeks [considered Gentiles], then to be fair, it would have had to include all gentiles, which means all of mankind. Anyway, we know for sure [no debating possible] that God was marrying some group of people, which included Paul and the church at Corinth, at the Passover sacrifice of Jesus. The "us" is still a mystery at this point.

If we are able to find out whom Jesus represented on this earth, then we will know whom He represented on the cross, which would give us the answer to the question of who the "bride" was in this Passover. It appears from my research that Jesus represented all of mankind, even though He was sent only to the Hebrews. We will look at a few verses which clarify this for us.

We can start with the covenant that God made with Eve in Genesis 3:15-16, saying that her Seed [Jesus] was going to take care of Satan. These verses could only be construed as representative of all mankind because the Hebrew nation was not around at this time. Still in Genesis and moving to the most important Old Testament character [including Moses], we see the covenant with Abraham and his Seed meant that all the families of the earth would be blessed by the Seed [Jesus].

Genesis 18:18 says that all the nations shall be blessed in Him, not just one [Hebrew] nation, but all nations, certainly referring to Jesus representing them on the cross. Psalms 72 speaks of Jesus [Messiah] representing all the people.

The clincher for me, and perhaps for you, is Isaiah Chapter 53. From my studies this is the chapter that divides Christianity from Judaism. The Hebrews refused to accept this chapter as referring to Jesus. Christianity takes this chapter as referring to Jesus and applies it to themselves. If it is true that this chapter applies to the Christian, it is also true that the verse applies to all of mankind, due to the fact that there were no Christians around when this chapter was fulfilled at the death and burial of Jesus.

Preposterous?! How can it be that it would apply to all of mankind and not just Christians? The answer is simple. We must again apply the covenanting principle laid out in Galatians 3:15, that once a covenant is confirmed, no one can annul or add to it. By following this universal covenanting principle, we find that Isaiah 53 must apply to all of mankind, if it applies to anyone at all.

In the New Testament, we find that "she will bring forth a son and you shall call his name Jesus for He will save His people from their sins." (Matthew 1:21) A true statement, whether pertaining to only Judah, or Judah and Israel, or all of mankind. Whatever the category, we know he saved them from their sins, "for the son of man has come to save that which was lost, for even the son of man did not come to be served but to serve and to give His life a ransom *for many*." (Mark 10:45) "Behold the Lamb of God who takes away the sin *of the world!*" (John 1:29) "...Christ, the Savior *of the world*." (John 4:42)

"For when we were still without strength in due time Christ died for the ungodly." (Romans 5:6) "But God demonstrates His own love toward us in that while we were still sinners Christ died for us." (Romans 5:8) "For when we were enemies we were reconciled to God through the death of His Son..." (Romans5:10) "Therefore, as through one man's offense judgment came to all men resulting in condemnation, even so through one man's righteous act, the free gift came to all men..." (Romans 5:18)

"He who did not spare His own son, but delivered Him up for us all..." (Romans 8:32) "...it is Christ who died and furthermore is also risen who is even at the right hand of God who also makes intercession for us." (Romans 8:34) "For if their casting away is the reconciling of the world..." (Romans 11:15) "For God has committed them all to disobedience that He might have mercy on all, oh the depth of the riches, both of the wisdom and knowledge of God! How unsearchable are His judgments and His ways past finding out!" (Romans 11:32-33) "...that Christ died for our sins according to the scriptures." (I Corinthians 15:3)

"...even so, in Christ all shall be made alive," (I Corinthians 12:22) "...that if One died for all, then all died; and He died for all..." (II Corinthians 5:14b-15a) "That is that God was in Christ reconciling the world to Himself." (II Corinthians 5:19) "For He made Him who knew no sin to be sin for us..." (II Corinthians 5:21a) "Who gave Himself for our sin..." (Galatians 1:4) "...according to His good pleasure which He purposed in Himself that in the dispensation of the fullness of times He might gather together in one all things in Christ both which are in heaven and which are on earth - in Him." (Ephesians 1:9b-10)

"And by Him to reconcile [fully] all things to Himself by Him." (Colossians 1:20) "And you who once were alienated and enemies in your mind by wicked works, yet now He has reconciled [fully]." (Col. 1:21) "...because we trust in the living God who is the savior of all men..." (I Timothy 4:10) "But when the kindness and the love of God our savior toward man appeared." (Titus 3:4)

"When He had by Himself purged our sins..." (Hebrews 1:3) "...that He, by the grace of God, might taste death for everyone." (Hebrews 2:9) "Therefore in all things He had to be made like His brethren that He might be a merciful and faithful high priest in things pertaining to God to make propitiation for the sins of the people." (Hebrews 2:17)

"Who does not need daily as those high priests to offer up sacrifices, first for His own sins and then for the people's, for this He did once for all when He offered up Himself." (Hebrews 7:27) "Not with the blood of goats and calves, but with His blood He entered the Most Holy Place once for all, having obtained eternal redemption." (Hebrews 9:12)

"Therefore, it was necessary that the copies of the things in the heavens should be purified with these but the heavenly things themselves with better sacrifices than these for Christ has not entered the holy places made with hands which are copies of the true, but into the heaven itself, now to appear in the presence of God for us. Not that He should offer Himself often as the high priest enters the Most Holy Place every year with the blood of another - He then would have had to suffer often since the foundation of the world; but now, once at the end of the ages, He has appeared to put away sin by the sacrifice of Himself...so Christ was offered once to bear the sins of many..." (Hebrews 9:23-26, & 28a)

"But this man, after He had offered one sacrifice for sins forever, sat down at the right hand of God,"

(Hebrews 10:12) "Who Himself bore our sins in His own body on the tree..." (I Peter 2:24) "For Christ also suffered once for sins, the just for the unjust..." (I Peter 3:18a) "Therefore, since Christ suffered for us in the flesh..." (I Peter 4:1a) "And He, Himself is the propitiation for our sins and not for ours only, but also for the whole world." (I John 2:2)

"And you know that He was manifested to take away our sins..." (I John 3:5) "By this we know *agape* because He laid down His life for us..." (I John 3:16) "And this is *agape*, not that we *agaped* God, but that He *agaped* us and sent His son to be the propitiation for our sins." (I John 4:10) "And we have seen and testify that the Father has sent the Son as Savior of the world." (I John 4:14)

Please excuse me for over stating my case, but I believe in founding my beliefs on insurmountable evidence. That is what I have just done, having listed every verse I could find to support the conclusion to the aforementioned discussion about Jesus as our Passover. The conclusion has to be that the "bride" in this Passover marriage was all of mankind and not a small group of mankind, such as Hebrews or Christians. If this conclusion is valid, then Protestant theology must be re-evaluated and changed accordingly. Either we are going to accept what the Word says, or we are going to continue teaching the traditions handed down from the Catholic church, by way of Martin Luther.

Now that the subject of Jesus as our Passover has been covered, we can get on with our discussion of the eternal covenant. We have established the fact that Jesus' blood was the Passover for the whole world and that there was a covenant being made at the cross, but we still do not know a whole lot about it. Following are verses that will give us more answers.

"Behold the days are coming," says the Lord, "when I will make a new covenant with the house of Israel and with the house of Judah - not according to the covenant that I made with their fathers in the day that I took them by the hand to bring them out of the land of Egypt. My covenant which they broke though I was a husband to them," says the Lord.

"But this is the covenant that I will make with the house of Israel: After those days," says the Lord, "I will put my laws in their minds and write it on their hearts; and I will be their God and they shall be my people."

"No more shall every man teach his neighbor, and every man his brother saying, "Know the Lord," for they all shall know me from the least of them to the greatest of them," says the Lord. "For I will forgive their iniquity, and their sins I will remember no more." (Jeremiah 31:31-34)

Looking back to Jeremiah's time, we see that God is going to make, or has already made, a new covenant with the house of Israel. He does not say when, but from the characteristics associated with the covenant, we may be able to determine the time. The writer of Hebrews uses the same passage to talk about a new covenant.

> "But now He [Jesus] has obtained a more excellent ministry inasmuch as He is also mediator of a better covenant which was established on better promises. For if that first covenant had been faultless, then no place would have been sought for a second. Because finding fault with them, He says, "Behold the days..." (vs.13) In that He says, "a New Covenant, He has made the first obsolete. Now, what is becoming obsolete and growing old is ready to vanish away." (Hebrews 8:6-13)

> "And inasmuch as He was not made priest without an oath [Ancient custom of promising to someone

to do something then calling on the gods to bring a curse upon the person if it was not fulfilled. Similar to a covenant, including the curse, but without the blood and no other party need be involved, a very, very serious pledge.] for they have become priests without an oath, but He with an oath by Him who said to Him, 'the Lord has sworn and will not relent, you are a priest forever according to the order of Melchizedek.' By so much more, Jesus has become a surety of a better covenant." (Hebrews 7:20-22)

"But Christ came as High Priest of the good things to come with a greater and more perfect tabernacle not made with hands, that is not of this creation. Not with the blood of goats and calves but with His own blood, He entered the Most Holy Place once for all, having obtained eternal redemption. For if the blood of bulls and goats and the ashes of a heifer sprinkling the unclean sanctifies for the purifying of the flesh, how much more shall the blood of Christ, who through the eternal spirit offered Himself without spot to God purge your conscience from dead works to serve the living God?"

"And for this reason He is the mediator of the new covenant [Greek *diatheke*], by means of death, for the redemption of transgressions under the first covenant [*diatheke]*, that those who are called may receive the promise of the eternal inheritance. For where there is a testament [*diatheke]* there must also of necessity be the death of the testator. For a testament [*diatheke*] is in force after men are dead since it has no power at all while the testator lives. Therefore not even the first covenant [*diatheke*] was dedicated without blood." (Hebrews 9:11-18)

In review, we see that Jesus became the mediator of a new and better covenant founded on better promises. When this new covenant came into effect [when it was confirmed], the old, or first covenant, was no longer in effect [vanished away - Greek *aphanismos* -used to describe laws that become out of date or abolished - Dake's Annotated Bible]. By an oath, He became an eternal priest [forever] and once for all entered the Most Holy Place and with His own blood obtained eternal redemption. Then it goes on to say that He was the testator of this will [*diatheke*], or covenant.

Since Jesus obtained eternal redemption and is a priest forever [etcrnal], it is obvious that Jesus was the person who made the eternal covenant with God for us. We [mankind] did not make the covenant so are therefore not under the obligation of the covenant. Only the two parties, Jesus and God, are under the requirements of the covenant. Keep in mind, this was a man's covenant, because Jesus was a man, so no one can add to, or take away from the covenant made at that point in time.

There is still more to learn about this covenant. It appears that the covenant with Abraham was also made with Christ:

"That the blessings of Abraham might come upon the Gentiles in Christ Jesus, that we might receive the promise of the spirit through faith...now to Abraham and his seed were the promises made. He does not say, 'and to seeds.' As of many but as of one, 'And to your seed,' who is Christ. And this I say, that the law which was 430 years later cannot annul the covenant that was confirmed before by God in Christ, that it should make the promise of no effect."

"For if the inheritance is of the law, it is no longer of promise. But God gave it to Abraham by promise. What purpose then does the law serve? It was added because of transgressions, until the Seed should come to whom the promise was made and it was appointed through angels by the hand of a mediator." (Galatians 3:14-19)

The blessings of Abraham came to the gentiles through the promises God gave to Abraham and his Seed, Christ Jesus. So, actually this eternal covenant we have at which we have been looking is connected to Abraham's covenant but it is not the same covenant. In the Abrahamic covenant the blessings for Abraham were that he would be a father of many nations. (Genesis 17:4) His seed will be as the sands of the seashore and possess the gates of his enemies (Genesis 22:17), and in his seed all of the nations of the earth will be blessed. (Genesis 22:18)

Keep in mind that Abraham had to remain faithful to his end of the agreement. He had to do what was commanded of him. "For I have known him in order that he may command his children and his household after him that they keep the way of the Lord to do righteousness and justice that the Lord may bring to Abraham what he had spoken to him." (Genesis 18:19)

He also had to do whatever else was demanded [NT "asked"] of him by his covenant partner, because he loved him so much that he would never require [NT "ask"] anything that would be too demanding, even to the point that he was required to sacrifice his own son on the altar. [To the oriental father this was the ultimate demand.] When Abraham was in the act of killing his only son, Isaac, he was simply acting as a "covenant friend," as was customary throughout the world at that time. That is not to suggest that his act was any small thing.

Now, look at the flip side of this [as Ken Copeland explained in his "Blood Covenant" cassette series]. Abraham had the right to demand of his covenant partner the same sacrifice, the sacrifice of God's own Son, and God, being a covenant keeping God, was obligated to offer up His Son when it was demanded of Him.

All parties in this covenant held up their end of the deal. Abraham did righteousness and justice, taught it to his descendants, and willingly offered his son as a sacrifice. God held up his end, by Abraham's descendants being innumerable, by offering up His Son when required, and by Jesus Christ blessing all the nations of the world.

Even with seeing a connection to Abraham's covenant, the eternal covenant [Jesus' covenant] is still too much of a mystery. So we are going to look at a large number of verses that would be considered characteristics of this covenant.

"Father, I desire that they also whom you gave me may be with me where I am that they may behold my glory which you have given me. For you loved me before the foundation of the world." (John 17:24) "...just as He chose us in Him before the foundation of the world, that we should be holy and without blame before him in love." (Ephesians 1:4)

"...although the works were finished from the foundation of the world." (Hebrews 4:3) "He would have had to suffer often since the foundation of the world; but now once at the end of the ages He has appeared to put away sin by the sacrifice of Himself." (Hebrews 9:26) "He indeed was fore ordained before the foundation of the world, but was manifest in these last times for you." (I Peter 1:20)

It was decided before the foundation of the world [see Dake's definition] that certain requirements were to be made of the Christ [Messiah - Anointed One]. In several places in the Old Testament, it is told [prophesied] about what the Messiah would have to go through, in other words, for purposes of our discussion, requirements of the covenant. The writer of Hebrews, quoting

Psalms 40:6-8, says about the Messiah, "Sacrifices and offering you did not desire, But a body you have prepared for me. In burnt offerings and sacrifices for sin you had no pleasure. Then I said, 'Behold I have come - in the volume of the book it is written of me - to do your will, O God.'"

It is obvious that Jesus had the understanding early in life that He had to be about His Father's business [Luke 2:49]. He was on the earth to do the will of God. Jesus, as a boy, according to the custom, was circumcised the eighth day, which brought Him into the Abrahamic covenant with its requirements, blessings, and cursings. Keep in mind that following the principles of covenanting, we know that anyone coming into this covenant will receive the blessings as long as they abide by the laws of the covenant. If they keep the laws of some other covenant, they cannot expect to receive the blessings of this covenant. The characteristics of a covenant must be taken as a group and must never be separated!!

By studying the Gospels, we see that most of the Hebrews living in Jesus' time had forgotten about, or were not abiding by the Abrahamic covenant. Check out the verses mentioning Abraham and you will see this to be true. Jesus, however, believed in and followed the requirements of that covenant.

According to Paul, Jesus was also born under another covenant, the Mosaic covenant. "But when the fullness of time had come God sent forth His son born of a woman born under the law." (Galatians 4:4) A different covenant meant different laws. The Mosaic covenant, or Siniatic covenant was a tough covenant to abide by. That is obvious because the Hebrews had broken this covenant centuries before. We know that, because the curses of the covenant had come upon them. Therefore, God was no longer under obligation to this covenant.

157

If God was no longer under obligation to this covenant, then why were all those Hebrews and Gentile proselytes still attempting to keep the law of Moses? That is a very good question! They had strayed so far away from the knowledge of what a covenant was, that what Jesus told them, and did among them, astounded them. Their ancestors that had crossed the Jordan into Canaan would not have been impressed at all. They probably would have said, "Big deal!" Miracles, and living in covenant with the God of this universe was everyday stuff to them at that time!

In Jesus' day, they were strangers from the covenants. That is why Jesus told them to repent [change your thinking] and believe in the covenant [gospel]. Jesus knew the covenant and walked in it. All they had to do was believe in the gospel [covenant] and walk in it and they would not have been in the problems they were in. [Gospel and covenant can be used interchangeably. Galatians 3:8 - God preached the gospel to Abraham. What did He preach, if not the covenant?]

What was God's position at this period in time when Jesus was on the earth? According to covenant principles, we know that He was not under obligation to the Siniatic Covenant, but He was under obligation to the Abrahamic Covenant, with anyone keeping the requirements of it. [Forget the Davidic Covenant for now.] Well, if God was no longer under obligation to the Mosaic covenant, then why all the typology [Jesus representing, or being a type of something in the Old Testament] and the interconnection with Jesus's death and things in the law?

An obligation to do something and a desire to do something are two different things. God desired to do things that way for the benefit of the people who clung so tightly to the law of Moses. It was not for the benefit of anyone outside of the law, unless for better understanding.

But, why was God still associating with these descendants of covenant breakers? Because of their faith! He was honoring their faith, not honoring their performance of the law! God has always honored faith no matter how ignorant the person.

Jesus was not under obligation to keep the laws of Moses. He was only obligated to keep the laws of the Abrahamic Covenant which were not as strict, but led to the same objective: love and justice. That does not mean that Jesus did not abide by the law of Moses. I have been unable to find any evidence that He was guilty of any infraction. The only thing I can find is His rebellion against the traditions surrounding that law. It was certain that Jesus never trespassed a law, or requirement, of any covenant to which He was obligated. If He had, then He would not have been the perfect sacrifice. [How do you think the first Adam got us into this mess?]

Where does this information lead us? Back to the Bible to interpret it correctly! It will give us more insight into Jesus' status during his life. But, we still need to look at the Old Testament prophecies about the Messiah. We know that He knew that He had come to do the will of God, and it appears that the will of God was to fulfill prophecy.

We need to understand though, that in order for Him to fulfill these prophecies, which could be considered requirements of a covenant, there had to be one of two possibilities. There either had to be a very strong desire on Jesus' part to be tortured and separated from God for three days, or there was a covenant involved.

The Abrahamic and Mosaic Covenants were basically the same for everyone involved in them. Although these were different categories with different requirements for priests, men, women, aged, nationality, etc. There were more general covenants pertaining to large numbers of people, whereas there were other covenants made in the Old Testament which were individual or lineage [Davidic] covenants. These followed the covenanting principle in that they only pertained to the parties cutting [making] the covenant or their descendants, as in David's covenant.

This point is important to understand so that there is no question about God doing something out of the ordinary in His dealing with mankind. He has always dealt with mankind by covenants from day six of His creation, and this talk about God dealing with mankind according to dispensations is nonsense!

From God's standpoint He did not need to have these covenants, in particular, Jesus' covenant, but it was for the purpose of giving mankind something to see, feel, taste, smell, or hear, so that there would be no question, because God could swear an oath, or oaths, for eternity and there would still be some doubt in the minds of some. After all, that was a common practice in Bible times, to swear an oath before God to do something. Speaking an oath is "strong medicine," but signing that oath in the blood of a covenant was the strongest statement that could be made throughout the history of the world. So, this was what God chose to do, not so that He would remain faithful to the covenant, but, so that mankind would know that a covenant was in force.

An oath would have worked for God, but He had to let mankind know that He had obligated Himself to a covenant with mankind, and as history shows, He is a covenant-keeping God. "Therefore know that the Lord your God, He is God, the faithful God who keeps covenant and mercy for a thousand generations with those who love Him and keep His commandments." (Deut. 7:9) Old covenant, but still accurate.

Mankind up until recent history was very familiar with blood covenants and accepted them as sacred and binding until death. So really, all God was doing, by using blood covenants, was using the most universally accepted method to show that He had obligated Himself to do something in regard to mankind. But, still we have not discovered exactly what that was.

Now, I am going to do my best to pull this all together so that the eternal covenant will be clear. We have to keep in mind that Jesus knew from childhood that He was to be the Messiah, which meant that all the Messianic prophecies of the Old Testament applied to Him, both the good and the not so good. He knew Psalm 2 and 45, as well as He knew Psalm 22. He knew Isaiah Chapters 52, 54, 55, and 56 as well as He knew Isaiah Chapter 53. And He knew that the world would see that He had made an eternal covenant with God on behalf of mankind. Once it was made and confirmed, no one could change it, no matter what they did. Only He and God had a right to change it, but even that was out of the question because once the blood was shed, no more mediation was possible. Any deviation would bring the curse into effect.

Remember when Jesus was in the garden just before His betrayal, He said, "Father, if it be possible, let this cup pass from me." He was referring to the requirements of that covenant. He was acting human and trying to see if there may be a "plan B." Every other person would have done the same thing! But, He knew that God kept His word, and those prophecies were His Word.

The following shows to what Jesus Christ was looking forward:

Psalm 22 - "My God, my God, why have You forsaken me? Why are You so far from helping me, and from the words of my groaning? Oh my

God, I cry in the daytime, but You do not hear; and in the night season, I am not silent. But You are holy, who inhabits the praises of Israel. Our fathers trusted in You; they trusted You and You delivered them. They cried to You, and were delivered; they trusted in You and were not ashamed."

"But I am a worm, and no man; a reproach of man, and despised of the people. All those who see me laugh me to scorn; they shoot out the lip, they shake the head, saying, 'He trusted in the Lord, let Him rescue Him; let Him deliver Him, since He delights in Him!'"

"But You are He who took Me out of the womb; You made Me trust when I was on My mother's breast. I was cast upon You from birth. From My mother's womb You have been My God. Be not far from Me. For trouble is near; for there is none to help.

"Many bulls have surrounded Me; strong bulls of Basham have encircled Me. They gape at me with their mouths, as a raging and roaring lion."

"I am poured out like water, and all My bones are out of joint; My heart is like wax; it has melted within Me. My strength is dried up like a potsherd, and My tongue clings to My jaw; You have brought Me to the dust of death."

"For the dogs have surrounded Me; the assembly of the wicked has enclosed Me. They pierced My hands and My feet; I can count all My bones, they look and stare at me. They divide My garments among them, and for My clothing they cast lots."

"But You, O Lord, do not be far from Me; O My Strength hasten to help Me! Deliver Me from the sword, My precious life from the power of the dog. Save Me from the lion's mouth and from the horns of the wild oxen!"

Now, that is quite a serious consideration, but it gets worse when you look at the event described in Isaiah 53. This chapter, I conclude, is the most descriptive of the characteristics of the covenant that Jesus mediated for mankind. If we accept this chapter as such, and conclude, without a doubt, that it is describing the eternal covenant, then we must align our theology accordingly.

"Behold my servant shall deal prudently. He shall be exalted and extolled and be very high. Just as many were astonished at you, so His visage was marred more than any man, and His form more than the sons of men; so He shall sprinkle[1] many nations. Kings shall shut their mouths at Him: for what had not been told them they shall see, and what they had not heard they shall consider."

"Who has believed our report? And to whom has the arm of the Lord been revealed? For He shall grow up before Him as a tender plant and as a root out of dry ground. He has no form or comeliness; and when we see Him, there is no beauty that we should desire Him. He is despised and rejected by men, a man of sorrows and acquainted with grief. And we hid, as it were, our faces from Him; He was despised, and we did not esteem Him."

"Surely He has borne our griefs and carried our sorrows; yet we esteemed Him stricken, smitten by God, and afflicted. But He was wounded for our transgressions, He was bruised for our iniquities; the chastisement of our peace was upon Him, and by His stripes we are healed. All we like sheep have gone astray; we have turned everyone to his own way; and the Lord has laid on Him the iniquity of us all."

----

1. Here we see Moses sprinkling the blood of the covenant which is referred to both in Exodus and Hebrews.

"He was oppressed and He was afflicted, yet He opened not His mouth; He was led as a lamb to the slaughter, and as a sheep before shearers is silent, so He opened not His mouth. He was taken from prison and from judgment, and who will declare His generation? For He was cut off from the land of the living; for the transgressions of my people He was stricken. And they made His grave with the wicked - but with the rich at His death, because He had done no violence, nor was any deceit in His mouth."

"Yet it pleased the Lord to bruise Him; He has put Him to grief. When You make His soul an offering for sin, He shall see His seed, He shall prolong His days and the pleasure of the Lord shall prosper in His hand."

"He [God] shall see the travail of His soul, and be satisfied. By His knowledge My righteous servant shall justify many for He shall bear their iniquities, therefore I will divide Him a portion with the great, and He shall divide the spoil with the strong, because He poured out His soul unto death, and He was numbered with the transgressors, and He bore the sins of many, and made intercession for the transgressor." (Isaiah 52:13-53:12)

From my research, this is probably the main chapter of the Bible that separates the Christians from Judaism. The Christian says that Jesus fulfilled this chapter, and the Judaizers refuse to believe that it refers to one man, but rather refers to a people, or group. Then again, if we look really closely at what this chapter says we will discover that very few Christians actually believe what this chapter says. We have to analyze it closely to get a good picture at what some, or all, of the requirements were of Jesus' covenant.

When carefully analyzed, we realize how most

Christians have disregarded at least part of this prophecy. The question is, why? It is common knowledge that God has never let one prophecy that He has spoken Himself, or through a man or woman, go unfulfilled when the appointed time came. He is able to back up what He says He will do. History proves that! So, why is it that this prophecy of Jesus on the cross is so blatantly disregarded?

I have never come across any Christian literature which did not accept this section of Isaiah as prophesying Jesus' death, burial, and resurrection. Maybe, had they known that it was all part of a covenant sworn in blood, they would have been able to accept it in its entirety. But, then again, it is quite obvious that the understanding of covenants has been lost in the western world since the North American Indian had "civilization" forced upon him.

We have to repent [change our thinking] about Isaiah Chapter 53. We have to accept it for what it was, and still is, an eternal covenant of peace with mankind; the blood being shed was God's own blood in Jesus. How can we honestly deny this covenant concept? It is so obvious! Therefore, if we find that this covenant was confirmed, then we have to accept the fact that no man or woman can change it. It is an established fact!

However, my discussion of the covenant is not finished. As I said, we need to analyze this chapter more closely to see where we may have missed it. In verses 4 and 12 the words borne and bore [Hebrew *nasa*] mean to "lift," "bear," "carry away," "cast away," "ease," "erase," or "take away." The idea is that of one person taking the burden of another and placing it on himself as carrying an infant, or as the flood lifted up the Ark [Dake's, p. 743].

In verse 5, we see the word carried [Hebrew *cabal*]

meaning "to carry, bear," translated "carry a burden" in the Old Testament. The idea is that the full load is borne by the one carrying it, so that all others might be free of it. Also, in verse 5, the word "for" could just have easily been translated "because" the first two times it appears. In verse 4 the word "griefs" should have been translated as "sickness" or "disease," as it has been throughout the Old Testament. Now, with these added bits of information we can get a clearer picture.

According to the eternal covenant signed in blood, Jesus has borne our sicknesses and diseases and by Himself carried our sorrows. He was smitten by God [not by man] and afflicted. Jesus was wounded because of our iniquities [perverseness and crookedness]. By His stripes we are healed. And the Lord [God the Father] has laid on Him the iniquity of us all. [We did not lay the iniquity on Him, God did, past tense.]

He was oppressed and afflicted. For the transgressions of My people He was stricken [past tense]. It pleased God to bruise Him, and He also made Jesus sick [put Him to grief]. When You, God, make Jesus' soul an offering for sin, You are not going to forget Him, verse 11. And when You did that, God, You saw the travail of His soul and were satisfied, and knew, according to the universal principles of redemption, You could not demand any other payment to be made. You, God, knew that mankind stood justified because Jesus bore their iniquities. Because Jesus poured out His soul unto death, was numbered with the transgressor, bore the sin of many, He therefore made intercession for the transgressor.

What I have written about is all past tense. It is an established fact "that Jesus stood between God and man and received the blow of the sinner upon Himself. He took the punishment the sinner should have received." [Dake's, p. 805] Why is it that so many Christians find it hard to believe that at a point in time [around 31 to 33 C.E.], that the Creator of this universe, of His own free will, decided to penalize one man [Jesus] for the wrong-doing of all of mankind? Thereby, declaring everyone, who ever lived, or will live, not guilty [justified]! Just like that! Just that simple!

It was as if God stood up and said, "Hey, you guys! I don't have anything against you anymore! Whatever punishment you had coming to you I made this man, Jesus, take for you. You don't have to worry about me changing my mind, because it was signed in blood and you know what happens to someone who breaks covenant. Besides that, as further assurance on your part, I have taken myself out of the judge's seat so that you can be assured of a fair trail. Because, guess who has been made judge? Yeah, that's right, Jesus! The same guy who took your punishment is going to be the Judge at your trial! Can you beat a deal like that?! The Judge already knows that you don't have any punishment coming because you've already been declared not guilty!"

So, where is that going to leave our accusers? We know going in, that no matter what we did, good or bad, will have no bearing whatsoever on the outcome of the trial. We have already been declared 'not guilty!' Let our accusers bring up before the court every nasty thing we ever did, but we do not have to bother bringing up all the good things we did, because it will not sway the Judge's decision one way or the other. The Judge has already decided that we are not guilty of anything in this court.

The Judge and His Father have already set the rules and they can't be changed. Of course, our accusers are going to move for a mistrial because it is so obviously a stacked court, but God does not care. After all, as the old saying goes, God brought the bat and ball, we are play-

167

ing on His field, so He will make the rules. And the rules state that we are not guilty!

Now, if the first two guarantees did not get our attention, this third one will certainly do it for us because it is the most serious action He could take to demonstrate His position in relationship to us. As we are aware of trusts, [some states use a deed of trust for real estate transactions] we know it is a system whereby the lender does not hold the deed to the property, but rather it is entrusted to a third [neutral] party to hold until the debt is paid in full, at which time the deed will pass to the buyer. As long as the conditions [payments] are being met by the buyer, the lender has no right to step in and foreclose, or take possession of the deed. This system fairly protects both parties.

Another way that trusts are used is by people individually or as a group. They will put money or assets into the hands of someone else to handle for a period of time or forever. That other party makes all the decisions in regard to these assets. In our every day life, we have no trouble understanding this particular action. Because Jesus did everything that was demanded of Him, God rewarded Him by turning over to Him all authority in Heaven and on Earth. In reality, what God has done is turn over His entire creation to a third party [Jesus] to hold in trust until an appointed time.

Please, we need to grasp the seriousness of this action! To prove to the entire creation His righteousness [justice], His faithfulness, He has turned over control to a neutral party. Can you see yet what would happen if He were to violate this eternal covenant? God would lose it all! His entire creation that He has worked upon so hard: He stands to lose it all, if He does not live up to the requirements of this covenant!

We may be asking ourselves, would, or why would

a sovereign Creator bind Himself so strongly to an agreement so obviously stacked against Himself? But, we must see, it is not stacked against Him! It is stacked in His favor! He gets just what He always wanted since the time of Adam and Eve. How's that you ask?

To explain, we would have to explain what happened in Genesis 1:27, in God's creation of mankind. Wanting to create them in His own image, He had to put His own blood [life] in them. That is what the meaning of the word Adam is. It means "God's blood." So, Adam was walking around with God's blood [life], God's Spirit inside him. When God gave Adam a "co-equal partner" [Hebrew definition for "helpmeet"] in Eve, she also had God's blood flowing through her. This same pure blood would have been passed down to all their children after them, forever, since all born through Adam and Eve are God's blood children.

However, a problem arose when Adam and Eve transgressed a requirement of the covenant that they and God had made. Before this transgression, they were in spiritual oneness with each other. But, after the transgression, they were spiritually separated [Hebrew "die"] from God because the curse of the covenant automatically came into effect, as every covenant has its curse.

When they became separated from God spiritually, they could no longer have that close, intimate relationship that they once had. That is what God had desired from them and their children, just as any normal, loving Father does. You see, there was an emptiness there, someone was missing and it could not be filled by anything else. No matter how many worlds or universes God could build, He would not be able to fill that emptiness that could only be filled by getting His children back into spiritual oneness with Himself.

Of course, we all know about emptiness, because all

of God's blood children have known the same feeling. That is something that we know is missing, inside us, but we are unable to find out what it is. It is the same basic thing that God felt. No matter what we do to try to fill that emptiness, it is still there. God has seen us trying to fill it with hatred, love, wars, pleasures, sex, drugs, money, work, family, alcohol, governments, human blood covenants, religions, etc., but nothing has been able to fill that gap left by the result of what our parents, Adam and Eve, did.

But God does not hold these things against us, as we see He did not hold them against Adam and Eve. All we were trying to do was fill that emptiness that was inside. So what we did on the outside, was simply a reflection of what was missing on the inside. Now, can we see what God was going through?! God had the same emptiness, any loving parent experiences when their children are estranged from them. Just picture what He was going through with all His children estranged from Him, not just one.

That is why He set out immediately after the transgression to get His children back into spiritual oneness with Him. He was not acting out of anger. He did not set out to punish them. Oh, sure, He had to justly deal with and punish the transgression, but that does not mean He had to punish the transgressor. In fact, He never set out to punish the transgressor and any belief to the contrary is false.

We need to realize the situation immediately following the transgression. Punishment of the offender never even crossed His mind, as we can read in the account of Genesis 3. Sure, He made arrangement to punish the sin, but not the sinner. This idea of God punishing the sinner did not come from the account in Genesis, but came along much later based on false notions, which He never intended to portray.

Now, if you are following closely, you will already see that, if His children were separated from Him spiritually, and knowing that the Spirit is in the blood, then our blood became corrupted. Which, in turn, meant that all children were born spiritually separated from Him, meaning that we did not do anything at all except to be born, to come into that state of spiritual separation from God. The belief that God would hold that against us, to blame us for something Adam and Eve did, is preposterous!! It is not an attribute of a just God!

God had set up the system of spirit, blood, and genes, so He had to live by it. But, He had also set up a way to get His children back into spiritual oneness with Himself. We would be able to come back into oneness with Him, if we were able to get His Spirit back into us. That could be accomplished by getting uncorrupted blood back into us. The only way we could do it was by instituting the blood covenant. But, an ordinary blood covenant itself would not do. It had to be made with a man with uncorrupted blood, someone who did not have an earthly father.

That brings us to why God had to take on the form of a man. He put His blood a second time into a man by way of a woman this time. It would not have mattered to God if Mary was a virgin, a mother of eighteen children, or a prostitute off of the street. The bloodline [spirit] would not have been affected at all. The only reason He used a young woman was so there would be no question as to where the blood came from. We have to follow the blood!

Remember, God put His blood into Adam, who put his blood into Cain and Abel. Adam's spirit came in through the blood that God put in him. Cain and Abel's spirits were in the blood that they got from Adam. That's right! Adam put it there. God did not. God put

171

into mankind the ability to produce spirit beings, whereby each person's spirit came directly from their earthly father, which all leads back to God in the beginning. Why is it so hard to believe that He wants His children to experience the joys that He experienced with children?

Paul speaks in Romans Chapter 5 about all men being born separated from God. "Wherefore, as by one man sin entered into the world, and death [separation] by sin; and so death passed upon all men, for that all have sinned:... Nevertheless death [separation] reigned from Adam to Moses, even over them that had not sinned after the similitude of Adam's transgression..." (vs. 12,14) Then he speaks about Jesus being the second Adam, indicating that Jesus and Adam were, at different times, in the same spiritual oneness with God the Father.

How do you think God's son, Jesus, was able to perform so many miracles while He was on the earth? It was not because He was a good little Jewish boy. It certainly was not because of the ridiculous notion that He was God on the earth. Anybody that believes that never followed the blood. He was a man just like us! The main difference between Him and us, was that He had the advantage of being born in spiritual oneness with God, allowing Him to not have to deal with trying to fill the emptiness inside. The other main difference was that He believed in the covenant that He was part of, that He believed He had access to everything God had, and then He went out and acted like He believed it! [Most of us say we believe that all things are possible with God, but we do not bother to act like it is true.]

We have looked at the evidence that explains the eternal covenant. It should be totally understandable to you by now. One last point I want to cover is the reason why this covenant is an *eternal covenant*.

The main reason is obvious due to the fact that all

covenants are in force until one of the parties dies. Even if the covenant is broken, the curse remains in effect as long as is designated by agreement, which is usually for the length of the covenant breaker's life, or it may pass on to successive generations. The important thing to know is that the covenant is in effect as long as both parties are still in existence to honor the covenant. We have no doubt about the two parties of this eternal covenant. They will be around forever.

13

HAVE WE REACHED A VERDICT?

In the preceding chapters I have presented the main body of evidence which I have come across in my years of research. I do hope that the many points of undeniable facts and historical definitions have brought you to the understanding that I came to several years ago when someone confronted me with the fact of the eternal covenant. At that time I did not believe, and did not want to believe, that all of mankind had been forgiven by what Jesus did. I was about the last person in the world that wanted people to be forgiven by what Jesus did. I was about the last person in the world that wanted people to be forgiven of their sins without earning it. Vengeance was one of my strong points, however, my loyalty to God's Word was stronger than my desire for vengeance.

My reason for telling this, is so that there will be no question as to my motive for writing this book. Some people may have suspected a liberal bias on my part, but nothing could be further from the truth. Until age thirty, I never thought of another teaching than eternal damnation theology. When challenged with the facts, I had to make a choice between believing the facts, which I did not want to do, and sweeping away the facts, thereby suppressing the truth by dishonesty.

But, the facts were that Conservative Christianity had too many "holes" in its theology. There were too many gaps in our teachings and preachings that needed to be filled by rock-solid answers from the Bible, so that unbelievers could see that the God of this universe is not the God portrayed by Conservative Christians or even religion as a whole. If Christianity is the true way to a relationship with our Creator, then Christianity must be able to give people the correct answers to their questions.

What Conservative Christians have historically done is give "pat answers" that have been taught from one generation to another, without anyone questioning those "pat answers." The answers were from the Bible, but they had no definitive, or historical evidence on which to formulate their answers. It is not that the evidence was not available to each generation, because it was available, just as it is today. The only difference today is that we have the opportunity to operate the way that God intended for us, that is, with greater individual independence; which actually means being led personally by God's Holy Spirit in us.

But, were not previous generations led by the Holy Spirit? Certainly not in Biblical understanding because Conservative Christianity is still teaching the same basic theologies of Luther, Calvin, and Arminius, with few variations. There has been no variation at all in the "eternal damnation" part of their theologies, and those men are the ones who established the "new" Protestant way of believing in heaven and hell. Before them, there was basically only the Roman Catholic Church's view on the subject.

Why have we not questioned the traditional teachings of the Bible? Is it because we are too afraid that we may have to admit we were wrong? There is no shame in admitting when we are wrong. The shame is in not admitting when we are wrong. It appears the real problem is, that when people admit they made a mistake in Bible interpretation, it affects the interpretations of many people, because the typical Christian accepts their theology from what someone else teaches them.

This is one of the main problems with denominations. They are so "bureaucratically slow" in "righting" a wrong interpretation, that it necessitates the formation of another denomination, or group, with the correct interpretation. However, this new denomination falls into the same type of rut, which gives impetus to a new denomination with more understanding. The vicious cycle continues *ad infinitum,* until a group of people get together, not for the purposes of espousing a certain theology, but rather with different goals for which they are united. Theology, to them, is just a progressive understanding of God's relationship with man, and man's relationship with each other.

Unfortunately, we have seen few of these groups throughout history. Most theologies of denominations are still based on false beginnings and not based on Biblical truths. I want to demonstrate this by touching on a few subjects that are related to our subject of heaven and hell.

The Southern Baptist Convention was started for the purposes of maintaining the institution of slavery, hence split from the northern Baptists. If we check their theology today and compare it to their theology of 1845 when the split occurred, what we will find is a set of beliefs almost point for point the same today as then. Probably only a handful of Southern Baptists today would advocate slavery, but almost everyone of them would talk the "company line," when it comes to eternal damnation. If they questioned the "theology" of slavery, then why have they not questioned the " theology" of eternal damnation espoused by the same church ancestors?

One blatant example of this Biblical apathy is the belief of most Southern Baptists in the teaching of eternal security, or "once saved, always saved." This theology, from my research, was first espoused by John Calvin and passed on to the largest Protestant denomination. There is not one verse in the New Testament that specifically makes that statement. In fact, there are at least two groups of verses that specifically rebut this idea of "once saved, always saved."

These two sections are Hebrews 6:4-6 and Hebrews 10:26-29. The accurate understanding of these verses comes only with the understanding of covenants. In these verses we see the description of the fate of covenant-breakers. That is the only category of person spoken of by the writer of Hebrews. It refers only to those people who have had a close relationship with God's Holy Spirit, then turned their backs on Him. They can never again come into fellowship, thereby destroying the eternal security theology. Had Calvin and the Southern Baptists known anything about covenants, they would never have believed such a totally false theology.

On the flip-side of this teaching, we find the teaching under which I was raised. That is, that we stand in jeopardy every second of our life. If even the smallest, most insignificant, sin is committed ten seconds before the rapture, and the person does not, or cannot, repent, then eternal damnation awaits them. This very same scenario was put forth, by me, to my Pentecostal father when I was a teenager. His response was the above. Which theology is worse, "once saved, always saved, " or "standing in jeopardy every second?" Each one is false, according to correct Bible interpretation, but the standing in jeopardy is much worse because of the doubt and fear that a person lives under. In the knowledge of what Jesus did for mankind, there is freedom.

Another related subject that the Southern Baptists, and most of Conservative Christianity, have not understood is the teaching on the "age of accountability." This theology says that heaven awaits a child that dies before an undefined age, when they would have been held accountable for their acceptance or rejection of Jesus. I suspect that this teaching was derived from the Jewish custom where their children are considered to become an adult at age thirteen. The reason I can only guess as to the origination is because the New Testament neither mentions this subject, nor refers to this idea.

The idea could have stemmed from the false teaching of the Roman Catholic Church and Luther that condemned to Hell those children that were not baptized by water. They only believed this because they did not understand blood covenants. They did not understand that water was not important except for drinking and cleaning. They did not understand that it was the blood covenants that were important in understanding the Bible. In my opinion, the age of accountability teaching has been used by people only because they could not come up with any other explanation for the discrepancy exposed by teaching that everyone must be saved to get to heaven. The only way they could say that, and also say that God was a loving Father, was to invent a way that made God look somewhat reasonable.

However, a big problem with this teaching of the age of accountability theology is that these children could not have gotten into heaven, because their names were never written in the Lamb's Book of Life. Is it not true that Conservative Christianity teaches that a person must have their names written in the Book in order for them to get into heaven? They also teach that getting your name written in the Book is only accomplished by being saved. Well, if you can only be saved by accepting Jesus, and a person must be old enough to make the choice on their own, then how could a child get their name into the Book? They can only answer this question by inventing another theology that either speaks of God's foreknowledge, or the predestination of man. Both of these teachings are simply poor excuses for inadequate

Bible study.

What I found interesting in studying the subject of the Book of Life is that the Bible never does tell us how to get our names into the Book of Life. Isn't that amazing? Almost all of Protestant Christianity has taught something that is not found in, or even alluded to, in the Bible, yet they say that all their theology is based on the Bible. Can we trust anything they say?

Take for instance the basic Conservative Christian understanding on the subject of eternal, or everlasting life. Most teaching on the subject has been that eternal life is something that will be in the future after we die. However, the Bible contradicts this teaching. John 17:3 says, "And this is eternal life, that they may know You, the only true God, and Jesus Christ whom You have sent."

That verse makes it pretty clear that eternal life is ours when we come to know, in a covenant sense, God and His Son, Jesus Christ, whom He sent. Other verses that back this up are: John 6:53-56, Romans 2:7, I John 1:2, 3:15, 5:12, and 5:20. When we study these verses, we find that eternal life is in us. It is not something we will receive in the future as has been falsely preached. This little bit of knowledge also calls into question the "eternal damnation" theology.

Along this line, take for instance the case of persons born without the ability to understand the gospel. How could they make a decision for or against Jesus? How could they be held accountable for their indecision? Is a God of love going to damn to eternal fire the people who never had the ability or the opportunity to accept Jesus? What about the aborted babies? They have a spirit don't they? If they do not, then abortion is not wrong. But they do have a spirit that, according to Conservative Christianity, must answer to God.

The enormous missionary efforts of the last few centuries were made for the purposes of saving the heathen from eternal damnation. What happened to the people that never heard in the almost twenty centuries since Jesus' death? According to Conservative Christianity, all of these people who did not accept Jesus before they died will spend eternity in hell. How could a God of love and justice do such a thing as this?

To show the absurdity of this theology, I want to use this analogy. What would happen to the Chinese woman who died ten minutes after Jesus died? It would be a fairly safe bet that she did not accept Jesus as her personal Savior. Why would God send her to Hell? She never had a chance! How many millions of others never had the opportunity to hear that they had to make a decision for, or against, Jesus?

Conservative Christianity's response to this question is usually the false teaching that each person will be judged by what they have heard, or know. I say this is false, because nowhere in the New Testament does it say that we will be judged by what we know, only by the deeds done in the body.

What is it exactly that a person has to hear in order to be judged as having heard enough to make a decision? A dumb question, you think? Not really, when you consider the ridiculous statements of Protestant Christianity. They say that a person has to hear to believe, but they do not say that a person has to understand what he hears. Does that mean that a Spanish speaking person has to understand what he hears? Does that mean that a Spanish speaking person can be held responsible for hearing an English spoken gospel?

What I hope you have seen in this book are the many holes in the eternal damnation theology. The main message of this work is that Christianity has never based its beliefs on what the Bible says, but rather on what *someone said the Bible says.* What the Bible says about God is true, and we need to find out what it says, if we are going to represent Him on this earth.

I want to close with these questions. Think of the most important person in your life. Then think of what they could do to you that would make you want to separate yourself from them forever. If God loves us more than we love our own, then why would He do to mankind what we would not even do?

The two most important questions to be asked about this subject are very simple. Does the Bible say that Jesus paid the price for all the world's sins? If He did pay the price, then all we have to know is, did God, the Father, accept that payment for all of mankind, and, *if He did, then why can't we accept that payment as paid?*

BIBLIOGRAPHY

1. THE AMPLIFIED BIBLE, The Zondervan Corp., Grand Rapids, Michigan, 49506

2. THE NEW THAYER'S GREEK ENGLISH LEXICON, Henrickson Publishers, Inc., Peabody, MA 01960

3. THE NEW ENGLISHMAN'S GREEK CONCORDANCE AND LEXICON, Hendrickson Publishers, Inc., Peabody, MA 01960

4. THE NEW KING JAMES VERSION, Thomas Nelson Publishers, Nashville, TN

5. HANDBOOK OF DENOMINATIONS IN THE UNITED STATES, Frank S. Mead, Revised by Samuel S. Hill, Abingdon Press, Nashville, TN, (1985)

6. DAKE'S ANNOTATED REFERENCE BIBLE, Finis Jennings Dake, Dake Bible Sales, Inc., Lawrenceville, GA 30245, (1963)

7. STRONG'S EXHAUSTIVE CONCORDANCE OF THE BIBLE, Abingdon Press, Nashville, TN (1980)

8. THE NEW TESTAMENT IN THE LANGUAGE OF TODAY, William F. Beck, Concordia Publishing House, St. Louis, MO (1964)

9. THE BLOOD COVENANT, H. Clay Trumbull, Impact Books, Inc., 137 W. Jefferson, Kirkwood, MO 63122, (1975)

10. JESUS RABBI AND LORD, Robert L. Lindsey, Cornerstone Publishing, PO Box 311, Oak Creek, WI 53154, (1990)
For information on Dr. Lindsey's teachings contact:
HAKESHER, INC. 9939 S. 71st E. Ave., Tulsa, OK 74133 (918-298-2635

11. PRECIOUS MOMENTS BIBLE STORIES

12. GREAT RELIGIONS OF THE WORLD, National Geographic Society, (1971)

13. COLLIER'S ENCYCLOPEDIA, The Crowell-Collier Publishing Co. (1962)

14. BEYOND DEATH'S DOOR, Marice Rawlings, MD, Nelson Publishers, Nashville, TN

Daniel Schinzing...

... welcomes all comments about this book, except those which attempt to prove "Eternal Damnation Theology" with the Bible as the source. However, all critiques and/or corrections are strongly desired.

The only way that I can always be right is by knowing when I am wrong, so that I can make corrections. If you know something about this subject which I do not, you would be doing me a great service by sending your information to me at the address below.

Also, if you wish to order more copies of *Eternal Damnation on Trial*, you may do so either through

Impact Books, Inc.
137 W. Jefferson, Kirkwood, MO 63122

or direct **from the author** at 1-800-293█-8899.
Visa or Mastercard are accepted.

The author's next book, tentatively titled, "The Modern-Day Commandments" should be available in June of 1994. This book is a life prescription for all New Covenant Believers.

Daniel Schinzing
P.O. Box 2003,
Cleburne, TX 76033-2003

------------ N O T E S ------------

------------ N O T E S ------------

------------ **N O T E S** -------------

------------ **N O T E S** ------------

------------ N O T E S ------------

------------ NOTES ------------

FOR ADDITIONAL COPIES WRITE:

Impact Books

137 WEST JEFFERSON
KIRKWOOD, MISSOURI 63122

AVAILABLE AT YOUR LOCAL BOOKSTORE, OR YOU MAY
ORDER DIRECTLY. Toll-Free, order-line only M/C, DISC,
or VISA 1-800-451-2708.